WITH THE BRITISH CAVALRY IN 1914

WITH THE BRITISH CAVALRY IN 1914

Matthew Richardson

Pen & Sword
MILITARY
AN IMPRINT OF PEN & SWORD BOOKS LTD.
YORKSHIRE – PHILADELPHIA

First published in Great Britain in 2024 by
PEN AND SWORD MILITARY
An imprint of
Pen & Sword Books Limited
Yorkshire – Philadelphia

ISBN 978 1 39905 152 1

A CIP catalogue record for this book is available from the British Library.

Typeset in Times New Roman 12/16 by
SJmagic DESIGN SERVICES, India.
Printed and bound in the UK by CPI Group (UK) Ltd.

Pen & Sword Books Limited incorporates the imprints of After the Battle, Atlas, Archaeology, Aviation, Discovery, Family History, Fiction, History, Maritime, Military, Military Classics, Politics, Select, Transport, True Crime, Air World, Frontline Publishing, Leo Cooper, Remember When, Seaforth Publishing, The Praetorian Press, Wharncliffe Local History, Wharncliffe Transport, Wharncliffe True Crime and White Owl.

For a complete list of Pen & Sword titles please contact
PEN & SWORD BOOKS LIMITED
George House, Units 12 & 13, Beevor Street, Off Pontefract Road,
Barnsley, South Yorkshire, S71 1HN, England
E-mail: enquiries@pen-and-sword.co.uk
Website: www.pen-and-sword.co.uk

or

PEN AND SWORD BOOKS
1950 Lawrence Rd, Havertown, PA 19083, USA
E-mail: uspen-and-sword@casematepublishers.com
Website: www.penandswordbooks.com

MIX
Paper | Supporting responsible forestry
FSC www.fsc.org FSC® C013604

Contents

Acknowledgements

As with any book such as this, there are many people who must be acknowledged for their help and assistance. Clive Morris of the Queen's Dragoon Guards Heritage Trust, and Jeremy Burton and Colin Crabbe assisted with photographs, as did Voirrey Johnson and Robert Cull. My late friend Patrick Gariepy also contributed two images for which I am grateful. John Caley as so often before worked his digital magic to improve the quality of the poorer photographs herein. Hywel Jones at the National Library of Wales provided assistance with source material.

In 2013 I wrote a book entitled *1914: Voices From The Battlefields*. During the ten years of research which fed into that volume, I was fascinated by the accounts of cavalry actions which took place in this period, and felt that these deserved more detailed coverage. I also felt, on reflection, that I had not given the Yeomanry regiments the coverage that they deserved, and that this should be rectified in a future volume. Now, another ten years further on, I am grateful to Pen & Sword Books for giving me the opportunity to fulfil that ambition.

As ever, any errors in fact or interpretation are entirely my own.

Matthew Richardson,
Douglas, 2023

Introduction

In many ways, the campaign of 1914 in France and Belgium marked the high watermark of the horsed arm of the British Army. The cavalry regiments had enjoyed a golden sunset in the Edwardian era, their position as a social and military elite unchallenged since the Boer War. The vast open spaces of the South African veldt had seen mounted troops come into their own as fast moving mounted infantry, able to challenge the Boer Commandos on their own terms; indeed large numbers of new temporary yeomanry or mounted infantry regiments had been raised for service in that war, not just in Britain but in South Africa, Australia, New Zealand and Canada. So it was little wonder that in the military thinking of the first decade of the twentieth century, the central role of the horse in time of war was assured.

What was less clear, certainly from a British perspective, was what exactly that role should entail. For many observers another important lesson from the Boer War was that 'traditional' cavalry such as lancer regiments had behaved rather poorly. There was a body of opinion within the Edwardian army, which included Lord Roberts as commander-in-chief, and others such as Sir Ian Hamilton, which held that the role of the cavalry should increasingly be that of mounted infantry, with the rifle now supreme over the sword and lance. Even some career cavalrymen, such as Robert Baden-Powell (appointed Inspector-General of Cavalry in 1903) were of the opinion that the days of the charge with sword or lance were now over. During his tenure, Baden-Powell was successful in introducing reform of reconnaissance training for the cavalry, with the result that their scouting abilities were much greater than those of rival continental mounted forces. However, this push towards reform of the cavalry was resisted by prominent officers such as Sir Douglas Haig and Sir John French, who believed that horse-mounted troops still held a role as a shock arm in modern warfare. With the retirement of Roberts, the reforms made under his command were in a large part quietly undone; for example the lance, which had been relegated to the status of a parade item, was reinstated in the role of a front line weapon. Evidence of the push back against the reformers can be found in the revised manual Cavalry Training 1907 which stated:

> It must be accepted as a principle that the rifle, effective as it is, cannot replace the effect produced by the speed of the horse, the magnetism of the charge and the terror of cold steel. For when opportunities for mounted action occur, these characteristics combine to inspire such dash, enthusiasm and moral ascendancy that that cavalry is rendered irresistible.[1]

The cavalry received a newly designed sword in 1908, and ironically (given that it was coming to the end of its life as a frontline weapon) it was the best and most carefully thought through pattern in the history of the British Army. However, one of Roberts' last acts had been to ensure that the mounted regiments also received a new rifle that same year – the Short Magazine Lee Enfield, which although it was to be the standard weapon across all arms, had been shortened by 5 inches and lightened by 1 pound in weight to ensure that it was suitable for cavalry use. General Sir Horace Smith-Dorrien (an infantry officer) made himself unpopular when he ordered cavalry officers under his command at Aldershot to practice dismounted action in the autumn of 1909, but went on to note that:

> The improvement in musketry was so marked that the cavalry went nearly to the head of the lists in Annual Musketry.[2]

New innovations such as the aeroplane, the motorcar and even the bicycle had not yet begun to challenge the supremacy of the horse in terms of scouting and as a 'shock' arm of the army. But the months of August to December 1914 would see those glorious regiments of the British Army come face to face with the reality of warfare that was becoming increasingly industrialised – and mechanised.

Yet it would be a mistake to assume (as many did at the time) that the cavalry, in order to be useful, had to be on horseback. Their mobility gave them an enormously valuable function as an emergency reserve, able to plug gaps or rescue perilous situations at very short notice; and when they were used in the trenches in 1914, their performance was often quite remarkable. Cavalry doctrine in 1914 and the Cavalry Training Manual 1912 put a very high emphasis on the cavalry's ability to operate in the dismounted role. There are numerous references to the high standard of marksmanship in the cavalry, and this is borne out by their successes in pre-war shooting competitions against the infantry; indeed a high proportion of cavalry troopers were first class shots. To pass out as a fully trained soldier, a cavalry trooper had to fire fifteen aimed rounds a minute at 400 yards; after two years' service a trooper was automatically tested for an extra sixpence a day Proficiency Pay, awarded for putting five bullets in a 4-inch circle at 100 yards. Further tests included firing fifteen rounds rapid into a 6 foot target at 400 and 600 yards. In 1912, Major General M.F. Rimington, Inspector of Cavalry in India, wrote:

> Our British regular cavalry are at least ten, if not fifteen, years ahead of any continental cavalry in rifle shooting, fire discipline, and the knowledge of when and how to resort to fire tactics.[3]

Even more than this they had a sense of élan which made them valuable soldiers even on foot. They believed that they were an elite force and this often translated into high morale, as many of their letters testify. At the heart of this lay the 'Cavalry Spirit' an ethos hard to define, but which held that the cavalry should always be ready to act independently and on its own initiative should an opportunity arise. Many years later, a former cavalry officer, Major General James Lunt, recalled that:

> A great cavalry commander, Sir Hubert Gough, once defined that spirit as a combination of independence of thought, quickness in decision, and boldness in action. I would choose to add one more quality – that gaiety of spirit which the French prefer to call élan – or even panache.[4]

In the British Army at this time, the infantry regiment was broken down into battalions, usually around 900 strong. The battalions served as components of various divisions, and the regiment as a whole did not take the field. The cavalry was organised somewhat differently. Each cavalry regiment was a self-contained unit, with no battalions. It was divided into three squadrons, each of four troops. It numbered some 600 men, though in dismounted action this number (and consequently firepower) was greatly reduced as one man in five was detailed as a horse holder to look after the mounts of his comrades, the so-called 'led horses'. The cavalry had advantages over the infantry in other ways however. The cavalry recruit was paid more than his infantry counterpart, was usually more intelligent, and often from a slightly better social background. Another measure of their quality was the high proportion of regular cavalry NCOs who were later granted commissions in the New Armies.

Officers were drawn almost exclusively from the upper classes, and had a reputation (derived in the public imagination from events

Although the simplified pattern tunics suggest a post-1914 date for this photo, it shows a squadron of cavalry on parade. The trumpeter is visible on the extreme left. Two troop sergeants stand in front of the men, with a squadron sergeant major to the fore. (Author's Collection)

like the charge of the Light Brigade in the Crimean War) of being brave but stupid aristocrats, with an affected air of studied amateurism and a suspicion of authority and training. However, Rimington was at great pains to stress the increasing level of professionalism to be found among young British cavalry officers of the Edwardian era, and maintained that the louche ways of the nineteenth century were a thing of the past:

> then, the pay was nominal, and the enforced work was ditto. Nowadays young officers begin work at daybreak and go on till midday, 1 o'clock, or perhaps till 3 P.M. The squadron officer is now training a succession of men for the Reserve. There is winter training, then squadron training, regimental, brigade, and possibly divisional training. The men are trained to a much higher standard, and they are trained now by the squadron officers and not

> by the adjutant and his staff … nowadays a cavalry officer does at least twice as much work as he did formerly, and that the cavalry officer not only devotes his life to a patriotic idea, but must also devote a large portion of his income, at least £200 to £300 a year, to the same purpose. The emoluments which he derives from the public purse are, if anything, less nowadays than a hundred years ago. The old type of cavalry officer, who joined the service for the amusement to be derived from it, is scarcer; but still he is to be found, and he faces hard work cheerfully and well. Against the discouraging influences … he has his esprit de corps and a fondness for the life, which is an open-air one, and in many respects an interesting one. For the first few years or so of his service an excess of book knowledge is not required, but it is desirable that the young cavalry officer should be able to express himself clearly in words or on paper, and this he must gain by thinking clearly. Let us consider his duties in those first years, and then we shall see what to teach him. The principle has always been maintained that it is right to work him hard when he first joins, and later he can drop into the pace of the remainder.[5]

Rimington maintained that it was essential to teach young cavalry officers to ride and to train a horse. A few officers could do this when they joined, and thought they were fit to pass out of the riding school at once, but this was not the case; they had next to learn to teach others. Again, many might have already thought that they could shoot, but musketry training was essential. The officer had to learn to groom and shoe a horse, and to apply simple remedies. He needed to learn the few main rules of tactics, reconnaissance, and scouting. He also needed to understand cavalry pioneering, and he had to master use of his personal weapon on foot and horseback. These skills were learned, not so much for himself, but so that he was able to instruct and be an example to others. He was taught the care of his men's health in barracks and on service. The young officer might even have been taught book-keeping, and he would certainly have learned something of household economics on the mess committee. He continued:

> But the high-spirited youngster whom we want, and who can leave the service when he wants to, must in some respects be treated like a blood horse, whom we feel we can guide, but cannot stop at a single stride's notice, as we could a temperate old horse. We must preserve his verve and desire to take the initiative, even if it occasionally leads him to do wrong, when we should remember the great legal maxim, 'If the heart is right,' and also our own youthful days. The addiction to manly, and especially to rough and dangerous, field sports must be regarded as an immense asset towards efficiency for war. Time spent in the chase, 'the image of war', must not be regarded as so many hours less given to his employer by the cavalry officer. We particularly want the hunting breed of man, because he goes into danger for the love of it. He must also be able to perform any of the diverse duties which he may be called on to carry out on service, such as to fortify a village, construct a pontoon, court-martial a prisoner, and so on. It is very desirable that he should have as much as possible practically taught to him.[6]

He summarised the sort of man the cavalry regiment sought:

> The really stupid man, who has no imagination, makes a very bad officer for training purposes, because in peace-time he is quite unable to picture to himself what does happen in an action. The same unfortunate trait makes

him a bad leader in war, because he is unable to picture what the enemy will most probably do in certain cases. In the cavalry this type of officer has no place, even in the lower ranks, because the cavalry officer so frequently has to act by himself, and then the fate of an army may be dependent on what he sees, or on the information which he sifts and sends into the chief. As an infantry officer of the same rank he is more under the eyes of a commanding officer. What, then, are the conclusions at which we arrive?

1. That we draw on a class who have not been used to much brain work.
2. That the young officer should be for choice country bred, fond of sport, a 'trier', and must have some private income.
3. That now he works much harder than he used to do, at first especially; but the work is, or ought to be, congenial work. His pay is the same as when he did little or no work in peace-time. So he is a practical patriot.
4. That his work consists largely of teaching others.
5. That many of the attributes which are most desirable, can be tested by no written examination.
6. That to recognize and do his duty is one of these. As regards this, much depends on his surroundings in the regiment which he joins.
7. That a cavalry officer such as he gets up to three to seven years' service, though he requires little book learning, requires fairly wide practical knowledge, also considerable powers of imagination; without these, his abilities for training his men and for leading them in war are likely to be defective.

> 8. Also that the main point which he must regard in all his training is not only, 'Is this a situation in which my command may find itself in war?' but also, 'Is there any situation in war in which my command is not practised?'[7]

One thing which was true across the board in British cavalry regiments was that the care of the horse came first and foremost, and certainly before the comfort of the men. Ben Clouting was a new recruit in the 4th Royal Irish Dragoon Guards in 1913, stationed at Tidworth barracks, and remembered:

> At 7am we left the barrack rooms to muck out the stables, cleaning out the wet peat and wheelbarrowing in new, dry rough cut peat distributed from huge loose bales. While straw looked nicer, peat made a better bed and could be evenly spread to a depth of six inches, to be topped up later to keep the horses comfortable. The horses were then taken for a drink and given their feed, hay throughout the week with a Saturday treat of bran mash mixed with hot water and a scoop of treacle. Only after the horses had eaten did we make our way to the cookhouse for breakfast, a couple of slices of bread, margarine and jam, or pozzy as jam was known, and a bowl of tea ... After breakfast, at 9am, a trumpet call signalled the start of training exercises, followed at 11am by another call for stables, when the horses were groomed and taken out for inspection by the troop officer. This was a thorough inspection, the troop officer wiping a handkerchief over the horse to check it was clean, then examining the saddlery hung up behind. At evening stables, we'd water the horses, before night rugs, old and fairly dirty blankets, were put on to keep them warm.[8]

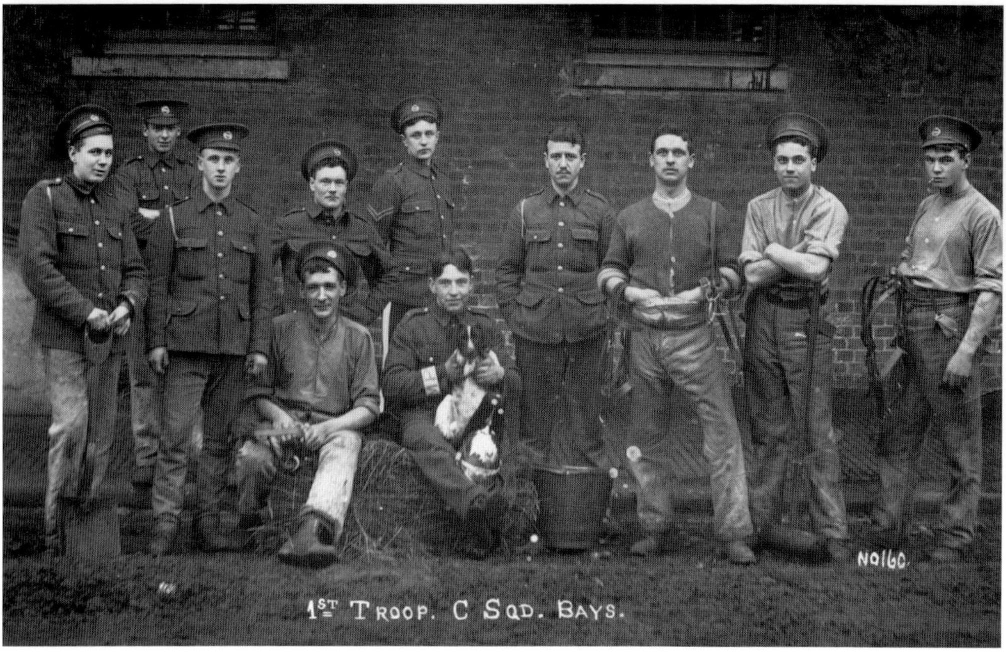

A group of the 2nd Dragoon Guards (Queen's Bays) engaged in cleaning stables at their barracks, around 1912. Note that the shirt sleeved men have braces down. This was common practice for men working with horses in this era, in case an animal should kick out and the hoof become tangled. (Author's Collection)

Of the four main cavalry arms which would see action in the western theatre between August and December 1914, that of the British was undoubtedly the most advanced in terms of training, horsecraft and equipment. Of the others, the Belgian was basically a force of civilians in comic opera uniforms; the French cavalry of 1914 also would not have looked out of place on the battlefield of Waterloo, with gaudy uniforms and bright breastplates. The firearms with which they were armed were also remarked upon by all who encountered them; 'a ridiculous popgun' was one apt description. The Germans, certainly before the war were much feared. Their Uhlans (lancers) carried a formidable reputation, but in reality the chief function for which the German cavalry was trained was a reconnaissance role. They lacked the capacity or training for direct battlefield shock action, to which the British cavalry aspired, and during the campaign itself were often described as timid.

This then summarises the character and position of the British regular cavalry in the Edwardian era and upon the eve of the First World War. The book which you are about to read analyses the performance of that cavalry in the crucial first period of movement in the war on the Western Front, and weighs the relative success of the apparently conflicting roles which they were expected to perform; at the same time it seeks to document at worms-eye level what it was actually like for them to ride in the saddle (and later stand in the trenches) in this period. In doing this, it draws where ever possible upon the first-hand experiences of those who were actually there, both from the regular cavalry and also from the part-time Territorial Force yeomanry regiments which joined them as the campaign progressed.

Chapter One

To War

The outbreak of the First World War found the components of what would become the 1st Cavalry Division in stations and barracks scattered across the British Isles. The mobilisation plans for the British Expeditionary Force (BEF) were detailed and comprehensive. Reservists were recalled from civilian life, gaudy full dress uniforms were returned to store, and additional horses were requisitioned. In peacetime, the number of troopers in a cavalry regiment outnumbered horses, but in wartime, every man needed a mount. The process then began of transporting the 600 or so men and horses of individual cavalry regiments to France, where they would assemble into brigade then divisional strength. Five brigades of cavalry went with the first contingent of the BEF; other units would join as the campaign progressed. Though the plans had been in place for many years, this did not necessarily mean that the process would be simple or straightforward. Second Lieutenant Roger Chance of the 4th Royal Irish Dragoon Guards was in training with his regiment at Tidworth as part of the 2nd Cavalry Brigade when war broke out. On 15 August 1914 this junior subaltern proceeded to France. He remembered:

> You try getting cavalry horses on to a railway train; getting cavalry horses onto a boat, into the bowels of a ship to transport them. [It's] no joke. We arrived in France, greeted by the French. We all went down to the south of Boulogne for a day or two, before we went off to the front. Right among the sand dunes we stripped off

> all our clothes, and rode our horses out into the sea. Then came this very tough [job], getting horses into railway trucks, eight horses in a railway truck, facing towards the centre. They kicked! As a young officer I had a pretty tough time ... We moved up to Mauberge by train, and got the horses out of the train there – this splendid cavalry brigade, commanded by General de Lisle ... Slowly we moved up to Mons.[9]

Squadron commander Captain Herbert Maddick, the 37-year-old son of a wealthy newspaper proprietor from London, crossed to France with his men of the 5th Royal Irish Lancers. Much of his duty consisted of checking upon the welfare of the horses, and then of the men:

6708 Trooper John James Hannah, 13th Hussars, seen prior to the war. A reservist, he was recalled to the colours in 1914. (Author's Collection)

Went round all the horse and troop decks. Dinner at 7 p.m. Smoked and talked; to bed at 11 p.m. Lovely night. August 16, Sunday – A lovely day; sea like oil. Got up about 6.30, after a cup of tea, and had a cigarette on deck. Only one bath on the ship, and that only cold sea-water. No fresh water available on account of the horses. Saw the horses watered and fed. Breakfast at 8 a.m. During the morning we paraded by squadrons, when the Colonel read the King's message, also K. of K. [Lord Kitchener]'s. Great enthusiasm over the former; men cheered like mad, Mid-day stables. Went round dinners – the men awfully cheery. After lunch smoked, read, and slept. We passed a battle-ship steaming hard for Plymouth; this is the first sight of the Navy we have had after being over twenty hours at sea. Looks as if the German fleet was 'bottled', as we have no escort. Evening stables. Had a chat with my N.C.O.s. Dinner 7.30 p.m., V. doing us well. An excellent dinner and Pommery 04. With coffee we opened a bottle of our 65 brandy – our table quite popular! We discussed the South African War, &c., after dinner. About 9.30 p.m. we were all rather startled by the report of a gun and the ringing of the engine-room telephones. Rushed on deck and found we were held up by a French destroyer, which played her search-light all over us. It was a weird sight, as the actual boat, though only about 150 yards from us, was hardly visible, as there was not a glimmer of a light on her. After having satisfied herself that we were 'all right' we were allowed to proceed to our destination, at present unknown, except to the Captain. Bed about 11 p.m. August 17, Monday. – Up about 6 a.m. to find we are anchored. The mystery of our destination is solved – it is Havre.[10]

The men and horses were soon acclimatised; morale was high among the men and the horses were in a high state of efficiency, once again proving the point that their care and welfare was of supreme importance:

> We marched to our Rest Camp at a place called Bléville, about four or five miles from the docks. A most inspiriting reception from the inhabitants. 'Vive l'Angleterre!' 'Vive la France!' and everyone begged for a 'souvenir'. Most of the men were minus their badges on arrival at the camp. After getting our horse-lines down and settling the men, the C.O. said a few very appropriate words to each squadron about their behaviour in general, and to the French army in particular. My men cheered him like mad – he is most awfully popular, and deservedly so.
>
> Most of us went into Havre for dinner and had a real good one at the Grand Hotel. As it was closed by martial law at 9 p.m., we were back in camp early and went to bed. Our mobilisation and transport over here have been more than successful; not a hitch anywhere, everything up to time and not a horse scratched.
>
> August 18, Tuesday. – Up about 6.30 a.m. and had a stroll round the horses; they look A1, and none the worse for the journey. An excellent breakfast at special tent run by an enterprising French-man, at a cost of two francs. Don't fancy he made much profit out of me. Sent the horses to exercise; no lameness. G. and I found a clover-field close by, and sent the men to gather a lot, and the gees had a good blow-out. Finished stables about 12. Went into Havre for déjeuner – excellent. Afterwards had a top-hole hot bath at the hotel – never know when one will get the next! 'Groaner' and I motored back to camp;

> called on the [Royal Scots] Greys on the way. Had a dish of tea with them. What a good lot they are! Did stables and then went to dinner at Havre. Back and to bed very early, as we start early to-morrow. I am the last squadron to entrain, and have to leave camp at 9 a.m. First squadron leaves about 4 a.m.[11]

The BEF was now moving up to take its position on the left of the French line preparing to meet the German advance through Belgium. No one was as yet aware of the juggernaut of enemy divisions which were coming towards the British, in particular Smith-Dorien's II Corps. The principal role of the cavalry was to be the eyes and ears of the army; scouting ahead to perceive the location of the enemy and reporting any potential threat observed.

Perhaps the furthest ranging patrols were those of the 19th Hussars. Its three squadrons had been split up, with one each providing divisional cavalry for the 4th, 5th and 6th infantry divisions. One of these patrols appears to have reached as far as Soignies. Through a wounded trooper, Mr W.E. Horne MP for the Guildford constituency later learned of the manner in which his son, Lieutenant W. Guy Horne of the 19th Hussars, was captured here, and made prisoner by the Germans. Lieutenant Horne was with a small party of his squadron, who were suddenly surprised by an overwhelming body of Uhlans. The wounded man, who managed to escape, reported that Lieutenant Horne had dismounted, and was making notes at the moment of the surprise. The last he saw of him was that he was emptying his revolver into the approaching Uhlans. Later, through the British Consul at Rotterdam, Lieutenant Horne, who was by then held in Westphalia as a prisoner of war, contacted his parents to report that he was in good health.

Just how effective the British cavalry were in this reconnaissance role is open to debate. On 21 August the Cavalry Division headquarters reported to GHQ that the German infantry was close by in great force. Apparently this information had been gleaned from French peasants, and was the product of a good deal of exaggeration. No actual German infantry had been seen by anyone in the Cavalry Division, and GHQ quite rightly dismissed the report as alarmist, caused no doubt by the sight of a few scattered Jaeger (light infantry) and German cavalry. Maddick certainly had not as yet seen any of the enemy in person. He continued:

> August 21, Friday. – Réveille at 3.30 a.m. Turned out. No bath this morning; it begins to feel like the real thing. Breakfast at 4 a.m. The old woman at the auberge made us coffee. Parade at 5 a.m. and moved off to join the regiment at Cousolre. We, the regiment, joined up with the rest of the brigade and marched to Bray. Nothing happened; no news of the enemy. March quite undisturbed. Arrived at Bray about 6 p.m. and went into billets. My squadron got quite a decent inn. After seeing the horses and men settled down, had a bath and then dinner, and to bed about 10 p.m. The men having a great time, as every village we went through the inhabitants all turned out and handed up beer, cigars, &c. They, the inhabitants, are more than delighted to see us, as they are terrified of what would happen if the Germans came. Those I talked to seem to hold the Uhlans in particular dread. Hope to goodness we have a chance of getting at these Uhlans and seeing what they really are worth. Of course in '70 they were never really tackled by trained troops, so it's quite on the cards they are living on a false reputation. Men all desperately keen on getting to grips.
>
> August 22, Saturday. – Réveille at 3 am. Our good hostess at the inn had hot coffee and petit verre ready. We added some 'bully' beef and bread, so had a good

> breakfast. It's a great thing to start the day with a good breakfast; one feels more contented and ready to take on anything. Stood to our horses until 6 a.m. This gave us time for an 'after breakfast' smoke and a good look round the horses and saddlery. About 6 a.m. we moved out and took up a 'position of readiness' on the higher ground about two miles N.W. of Bray. Squadron leaders went forward with the C.O. about three-quarters of a mile for observation, where we remained for some hours. There was an inn on the road, close by. The owners insisted on supplying us with bread, butter, jam, cheese, wine and beer, and absolutely refused to take any payment. Patrols come in reporting German patrols in the vicinity. As the children say, 'we are getting warm'. Ah! This looks like business. Shells are seen bursting over the village of Peronne on our right front, held by the 2nd Cavalry Brigade. The shelling becomes heavy, and we can see the village is on fire. The 3rd Cavalry Brigade (ours) is moved back to some higher ground S.W. of Bray, in line with and on the left of the 2nd Cavalry Brigade, which has fallen back on Binche.[12]

* * *

On 22 August Trooper Ernest Thomas, of C Squadron of the 4th Royal Irish Dragoon Guards, fired the first shot from a British soldier in the First World War. The unit was reconnoitring along the Mons-Charleroi road, near the Château de Ghislain, when an enemy patrol of Uhlans (or lancers) was first sighted. From German sources, the enemy patrol would appear to have been a mixed force from *Kurassier-Regiment Nr. 4* and *Hussaren-Regiment Nr. 8*. One troop of the Royal Irish was ordered to dismount and prepare their rifles, whilst another troop stood ready to charge with the sabre. Thomas takes up the story:

> I saw a troop of Uhlans coming leisurely down the road, the officer in front smoking a cigar. We were anxiously watching their movements when [suddenly] they halted, as if they had smelt a rat. They had seen us! They turned quickly back. Captain Hornby got permission to follow on with the sabre troop, and down the road they galloped.
>
> My troop was ordered to follow on in support, and we galloped on through the little village of Casteau. Then it was we could see the 1st troop using their swords and scattering the Uhlans left and right. We caught them up. Captain Hornby gave the order '4th Troop, dismounted action!' We found cover for our horses by the side of the château wall. Bullets were flying past us and all round us and possibly because I was rather noted for my quick movements and athletic ability in those days, I was first in action. I could see a German cavalry officer some four hundred yards away standing mounted in full view of me, gesticulating to the left and to the right as he disposed of his dismounted men and ordered them to take up their firing positions to engage us. Immediately I saw him I took aim, pulled the trigger and automatically, almost instantaneously, he fell to the ground, obviously wounded … at the time it seemed to me more like rifle practice on the plains of Salisbury. In one respect, however, and within a second or two, it was mighty different. From every direction, as it seemed, the air above us was thick with rifle and machine gun bullets …[13]

Thomas claims that with five prisoners taken (German sources state three), the objective of the patrol was achieved and they withdrew, not

5063 Trooper Ernest Thomas of the 4th Royal Irish Dragoon Guards who fired the first British rifle shot of the First World War, on 22 August 1914, on the Mons-Charleroi road. (Author's Collection)

having lost a single man killed or wounded. This patrol had indeed succeeded in locating (and identifying) enemy troops ahead, but the Germans who escaped also made a report, so it was very much a case of honours even on that score. More significantly, the withdrawal of the 4th Dragoon Guards left the countryside north of Casteau free for the Germans, and it was soon swarming with their cavalry. Later that same morning, a German patrol clashed with two squadrons of the Royal Scots Greys guarding the bridges at Binche and Péronnes. The Germans opened fire from a distance, and D and E batteries of the Royal Horse Artillery (RHA) returned fire in support of the Greys.

At about 11.30 am on 22 August the 3rd Cavalry Brigade came into contact with the enemy in strength at Péronnes and continued to clash with them throughout the day. Several instances of bold actions by small units were recorded, one example being that of Lieutenant Tempest Hicks, of the 16th (Queen's) Lancers, who when

> sent with a troop to clear up the situation near Péronnes, suddenly came upon about a company of Jaegers in a corn-field. He at once charged and rode straight through them. He charged through them again on his return

Men of the 16th Lancers, seen prior to the First World War. (Author's Collection)

> journey, inflicting heavy loss. His own losses were only two or three horses killed and several wounded. His own horse was shot under him.[14]

The 20th Hussars sent out patrols in the direction of Binche, one under Lieutenant Goodheart headed in the direction of Seneffe, some 10 miles north of Binche. The atmosphere was one of great excitement, the young officers of the regiment could as yet hardly believe that this was real war:

> Very soon… I saw on the road… a strong troop, about 25 men, mounted on dirty-coloured horses (resembling greys dyed with Condy's). They were about a mile away. My signaller tried to semaphore them with two service caps, but I was not surprised when they took no notice.

> I therefore left my patrol, and rode over by myself to 'liaise' with them. I got quite close to them before I realised they were carrying lances and were Huns. I returned to my patrol at a gallop. Part of the way lay along a pavé road running through a deep cutting. I looked round and saw an ugly Hun with a lance not more than two horses' lengths behind me. After that I gave my whole attention to keeping my horse on his legs on the pavé.[15]

To his embarrassment Goodheart tried to shoot the German with his revolver, only to discover that he had forgotten to load it. He none the less reached his patrol, which drove off the Germans. He returned to the regiment with three German horses; the enemy saddles and accoutrements created great interest, but the animals were judged to be of inferior quality.

That afternoon further patrols had been sent forward by the German cavalry. One from *Dragoner-Regiment Nr. 16* observed that the bridges at Nimy and Oburg were defended, but those further to the east were not. Another from *Hussaren-Regiment Nr. 8*. under Leutnant Schoeller reached the outskirts of Mons, and approximately half a mile in front of him through field glasses observed several Tommies in greatcoats guarding a canal bridge, whilst smoking and chatting to local children. The fact that a German patrol could approach the principal part of the British defensive position, and was able to report on enemy dispositions, without encountering any sort of mounted screen casts grave doubt on the effectiveness of British cavalry in this role.

Nevertheless, these first encounters notwithstanding, a force of Germans far larger and far more powerful than the BEF was now approaching at alarming speed. Both the French and British high commands had massively underestimated the strength of the German right wing, consisting mainly of General von Kluck's First Army. Field Marshal Sir John French, commanding the BEF, told General

Sir Horace Smith-Dorrien of II Corps that he believed only one or at most two enemy corps would be encountered. In fact seven corps were on their way. By early afternoon of the following day two German corps were actually engaged, with a third entering the fray and a fourth about to do so; indeed a feature of the Battle of Mons was to be the piecemeal way in which the German units involved came in to action; this to some extent negated the overall superiority in numbers enjoyed by the Germans, for the British were thus able to deal with each attack as it developed, before turning to the next. This time the British cavalry screen was on occasion roughly handled. A patrol of the 20th Hussars

Der erste gefangene Engländer (am Canal du Centre). Schlacht bei Mons, 23. August 1914

This remarkable photograph was taken from a German regimental history. It shows possibly the first British prisoner of the First World War on 23 August 1914. He is clearly a cavalryman, leading his horse, and may be from an ill-fated patrol of the 20th Hussars. (Author's Collection)

under Lieutenant Soames encountered a party of Germans; Soames was killed, one of his men was wounded and two were missing.

Unsurprisingly the next day the massively outnumbered British Expeditionary Force had no choice but to begin to withdraw. In the August heat, and with little in the way of food or water save what they could find on the way, the retreat was an exhausting one. For Maddick, his only brush with the enemy was some not particularly effective shell fire, but the day was still tiring:

> The guns are now turned on to the high ground. We see it getting hot. We are ordered to retire to the higher ground to our right rear, which means we have to cross a shell-swept area. We retire by troops and are well shelled, but no harm done. Men very steady and drill just as if they were accustomed to be shelled, whereas very few have ever been shot at before. Take up a new position, which we hold till about 6 p.m., not attacked. About 6 p.m. we retire and march to Elouges, W. of Mons, where we arrived at 3 a.m. on Sunday morning, going the whole time. Oh that march! Everyone dog-tired, and no food except what we carried on us.
>
> At one village 'Bossie', my interpreter, got some bottles of wine, which we did enjoy. We marched SE. of Mons, and for about ten miles over cobble-stones, very slippery, through what seemed like one continuous town, but of course in reality several, though they all joined. To judge by the crowds lining the streets they must be mining and iron-foundry hands. The whole way was one incessant roar of 'Vive l'Angleterre!' 'Vive la France!' 'Vive la Belgique!' and lastly, 'Vive l'Entente!' Oh! how tired and heartily sick one was of those cries!
>
> At last we reach Elouges and find two squadrons are crowded into a school-house, and 300 horses are to be

> picketed in the playground! and not a big one at that. Imagine it! Packing 300 horses into a yard that would not hold 100 in comfort. Every one beat to the world. I would shoot – no, torture – that billeting officer if he had been there. After a lot of trouble we get them all in, packed like sardines. We get in the schoolmistress's house, eat some 'bully,' and lie down on the floor and sleep, after twenty-four hours!!![16]

Nearby, at Elouges, the 2nd Cavalry Brigade was acting as rearguard to try to protect the 5th Division which was slow in withdrawing. In particular the 1st Battalion of the Cheshire Regiment found itself dreadfully exposed, the Germans outflanking it on both sides. Two other cavalry regiments, the 4th Royal Irish Dragoon Guards and the 9th Lancers made a charge here, in an attempt to halt the German advance and buy the Cheshires some time. The action has been described as heroic, though seventy-five years later Ben Clouting, who took part in it was less certain, stating that:

> It was a proper mêlée, with shell, machine gun and rifle fire forming a terrific barrage of noise … We were galloping into carnage, for nobody knew what we were supposed to be doing and there was utter confusion from the start.[17]

The situation was worse than chaotic as what had initially been ordered as a reconnaissance turned into a full scale charge, with orders passed from man to man, the whole thing gaining its own momentum. Second Lieutenant Roger Chance, the young subaltern with the 4th Dragoon Guards was present and recalled the exhilaration and adrenaline of the action:

> [I was] commanding a troop in A Squadron. The bells were ringing on Sunday 23 August in Mons. The people

of Mons were going about their business quite happily. We heard a few guns, and I can remember clearly seeing Major Bridges coming back with his squadron with German cavalry prisoners sitting on their horses, with their lances. They moved the whole of the 2nd Cavalry Brigade in the middle of the night, from the right front right behind Mons to the left, to hold the Condé canal, and we arrived, and that was when the really heavy German attacks began on Mons, and particularly the Condé canal on the left front ... [The next day] we were behind the village of Audregnies about noon, in a field dismounted. Shells were now falling on the roofs of the village. We prepared to mount – [gave the order to] mount – and off we went through the village ... I can remember clearly going through that village with my troop. To one side was Colonel Mullins, watching us go past with some apprehension no doubt, and C Squadron went to the left at the forward gallop, to seize some cottages and that was where Major Bridges was wounded and only just escaped being taken prisoner.

We formed column of troops at the gallop – 'Draw Swords!' – I rode at the head of my troop with my troop sergeant, a remarkable man, beside me. It was an absurd thing really. The harvest was just over, and this was a field. [It was a] terribly different country [generally] of mines and slag heaps, but this was open country, a field in which the corn was in stook. We went full gallop down a dusty road, or track, a column of troops. I wasn't aware of it but there were artillery shells bursting on us, a certain amount of rifle fire, but I never saw a German! There were some hidden behind the stooks no doubt.

First thing that happened when we went in at full gallop was my troop sergeant beside me, his horse was shot dead under him, he turned a complete somersault and

> I thought, 'well, he's gone'. He turned up later on a loose horse, alright. Remarkable man. We galloped on. I won't say that men were falling left and right of me, because that would be exaggerating, the losses were nothing like you would imagine. We came to a sunken road. The 9th Lancers were held up by wire, and got to a sugar factory which they occupied, but weren't able to do any more. I can very clearly remember Charles Norman, a subaltern of the 9th ... He was there, and there was a railway line going over the cutting, over a bridge. I saw loose horses at full gallop along that. I saw a man on a horse going at full gallop, a shell burst over him and that was the end of him. Well, we withdrew with our squadron, and we thought for a time that we were the sole survivors, because the rest of the brigade had been completely split up. I found then that I had got my troop more or less intact, not many killed or wounded. In fact, as regards other ranks as a result of that charge of the 4th Royal Irish Dragoon Guards was one officer killed and one or two wounded and taken prisoner. I don't think it was more than that.
>
> So A Squadron slowly withdrew when the Retreat began, withdrew wondering what happened to the rest of the brigade. It was a tough business, exhausting business, very little food or anything to drink, bully beef and so on. [The brigade] reassembled at Le Cateau, just before the Battle of Le Cateau started.[18]

Squadron commander Captain Francis Grenfell of the 9th Lancers wrote afterwards:

> We had simply galloped about like rabbits in front of a line of guns … men and horses falling in all directions. Most of one's time was spent in dodging the horses.[19]

A troop of the 9th Lancers, seen shortly before the First World War. (Author's Collection)

The squadron took shelter behind a house but very soon it was blown to pieces, so then moved off to the shelter of a railway embankment. Grenfell remembered that on one occasion the regiment had been ordered to trot in South Africa under a heavy fire, and he now adopted this method of keeping his men together. Under the embankment he collected the remnant. He found a number of odd 9th Lancers besides his own squadron, and as senior officer he took command and attempted to sort the troops out.

One of the enlisted men of the 9th Lancers present here was Trooper Harry Easton from Canterbury. He had joined the regiment in 1906 and was thus, like most of his fellow troopers, a highly competent horseman, but he remembered many years later that one of the finest cavalry regiments in Europe was brought to a halt not by enemy fire but by the novel feature of a barbed wire fence, and that the lancers galloped up and down the length of it like sheep, unsure of what to do next. Enemy fire was intense, and Easton's horse fell dead under him. Even after seventy-five years his memory of the events was vivid:

> We moved off under Sir David Campbell who gave the order 'Form Line of Squadrons', B Squadron on extreme right of the Regiment. On our right was one squadron of 18th Hussars, swords drawn, and on our left was one squadron 4th Royal Irish Dragoons [*sic*]. I remember very distinctly seeing the whole line at a hand canter … during this time the German artillery opened up and shrapnel was bursting overhead but they could not keep the trajectory of fire, it was always bursting overhead or behind. By this time about one or two hundred yards [on we] found ourselves confronted with a huge brick yard surrounded by a 12 foot high barbed wire fence. We were in to it very close when my horse fell and threw me – I'm not sure whether she had been hit or had stumbled, although the ground I remember was flat, slightly downhill & a small bump here & there. The CO signalled 'Troops Right Wheel' but it was not possible because we were in total confusion. There was no room left in front for such a move to be made by mounted men. There was a terrible mix up of Hussars and Lancers trying to extricate themselves. [There were] men, like myself who were dismounted, [who] had had their mounts shot from under them … I lay where I had fallen simply on account of heavy supporting fire from the Cheshire Regt who were covering our advance, which was abruptly brought to a halt by this barbed wire fence.[20]

A third account of this charge exists, in the form of a letter written home afterwards by an unnamed corporal of the 9th Lancers. It reads:

> We rode absolutely into death, and the colonel told us that onlookers never expected a single Lancer to come back. About 400 charged and 72 rallied afterwards, but during the week 200 more turned up wounded and otherwise. You see, the infantry of ours were in a fix and no guns but four could be got round, so the General ordered two squadrons of the 9th to charge, as a sacrifice, to save the position. The order was given, but not only did A and B gallop into line, but C squadron also wheeled and came up with a roar. It was magnificent, but horrible. The regiment was swept away before 1,000 yards was covered, and at 200 yards from the guns I was practically alone — myself, three privates, and an officer of our squadron. We wheeled to a flank on the colonel's signal and rode back. I was mad with rage, a feeling I cannot describe. But we had drawn their fire; the infantry were saved.[21]

A more detailed account was published in the *Croydon Times*, from Private Thomas Cotton of the 9th Lancers. It read:

> During our advance we came across large bodies of the enemy, and we said to one another, 'Now lads, we are in for a warm time.' We had no need to look to see if our rifles were alright, as a British Tommy classes that as his best chum. The order was passed round to make sure that every round found a resting place in the enemy. Our swords and lances were as keen as ourselves, and our horses were itching to get on the move. This particular day – August 24th – never will be forgotten by any man who was in this engagement. Our brigade was called into

860 Trooper Jack Linder, 9th Lancers, killed in action on 24 August 1914 and buried at Elouges Communal Cemetery. (Courtesy of Robert Cull)

action by the officer commanding the Infantry Division, and we had to go through a sort of lane to get into the open. We were allowed to get so far into the open, and when they thought that we were all out we received a very hearty welcome from rifle, Maxim and shrapnel fire. We had the order to form line, which very few heard, but it was done as if on drill. We went galloping on until we heard 'Line will attack', and then our minds were relieved when 'Charge' was given. Whether the 'charge' was sounded by the trumpeter no one can tell, but all I know is that we were in the thick of it.

The South Wales Borderers, The Royal West Kents, Loyal North Lancashires were waiting on our flanks, and they received a very heavy shelling. There is no need to repeat the damage inflicted on the enemy by the grand work of every regiment at Mons, as it was slaughter. The battle was a bit warm, considering it was the first engagement. I cannot express the feelings of our men in the charges, as they were all mad for the time being.

Their cavalry, even when in superior numbers, fly before ours. On one occasion I may mention a party of 9th Lancers numbering from 40 to 50, came in contact with a squadron of Uhlans, numbering about 250, in the open. Our men were let loose, and the way they went through the Uhlans, and back again, thrice repeated in a few minutes, was a credit to the British Cavalry. Our casualties were slight, but the enemy suffered severely. I was told a few days ago that a German prisoner told about this conflict, and it was the first time that the prisoner had been in action. He mentioned that he would rather face anything than face 'The 9th' and their lances 'as they are mad' He is still suffering from the effects. Nerves, lances and the 9th are before him in his sleep ...[22]

Meanwhile, the now rapidly advancing Germans soon picked up the unhorsed Harry Easton. He remembered:

> I was made to advance in the front line with the German infantry, [my guard] firing his rifle from the right hip while having frequent nips from his water bottle in his left hand which I learned later contained wine (I was not offered any).
>
> We had not gone very far before an odd cavalryman was picked up and a little further on we came across very many dead and a few sitting up, wounded – I recognised their cap badges as The Cheshire Regiment. Quite a lot of them were lying prone, having been shot and fallen on their rifles. Some, too, were face upwards – 'spreadeagled', not a pretty sight. We marched across country all the way till night began to fall and from what I can remember, and there were many of us too, we were ready to drop. We were fed at the same time and the same food as our captors – I was escorted by two infantrymen to a mobile cooker and was given a large bucket full of stew. I had gone a few yards with this towards a place where there were German infantry and officers and British prisoners, of cavalry and infantry, when a German soldier took my bucket of stew. Within minutes I had found [a] German officer … and told him about the stew – he took me back and I recognised the German soldier who still had the bucket. Without any preamble the officer knocked down the German soldier, kicked him up and made him hand over the bucket of stew to me.[23]

Another cavalry soldier taken prisoner here was Trooper Robert Waister of the 18th Hussars who had gone into action alongside the 9th Lancers. The Hussars had been given the order for dismounted action, so their horses had been led away to the rear. Advancing through a cornfield, German shells began bursting behind and scattered the regiment's horses. He was ordered to retire, but the horses had all either been killed or had bolted. Waister took cover with some men of the Cheshires beside a farmhouse, until it became clear that they had been outflanked and Germans were behind them. At this point the officer commanding the Cheshire soldiers told every man to make his escape as best he could. Waister also wrote of the events, many years later:

> [The officer] and many of his men dashed off to my left, but as Jerry came up around our left flank he would have to get through their lines so I decided for the right flank taking what little cover there was and a good many lads that had not made a move, but were taking cover behind the farmhouse followed me in single file, but I was on my own when I crossed open ground with no cover until I dropped into a hollow … but the Jerries' left flank had advanced faster than I thought and shortly after when dropping down into the roadway which led to the rail bridge collared by their advance troops marching up. They tied my hands behind my back and two of them escorted me back down the road from the direction in which I travelled and when we came to the road or railway bridge there was some ghastly sights of wounded and dead lying out on the bankside and a horse or two pulled to one side of the roadway after they had been knocked off the bridge.
>
> Then the main body of German troops started to march past and after a good many had passed a German officer leading his company shouted something to the two Jerries guarding me and they untied my hands which was sensible for I am sure that I did not look at the time

> like taking on the German army that was passing and shortly afterwards there followed with a strong escort of Jerries hundreds of British prisoners … to see some of my own Regiment among the prisoners was … a relief that they had been taken earlier than me so it had been a hopeless position for them also and as they told me (for some of them were from B Squadron) when going into action their officer Lieutenant Lawrence said to them 'I do not mind doing a bit fighting lads but I do object being a piece of cheese in a mousetrap' that coming from Posh Lawrence who gained the V.C. in the Boer War and was our Riding Master in peacetime shows clearly what we were asked to do; well I was put with those lot of prisoners and were marched towards the line the British and held that morning and many more wounded and dead were laid out where they had been fighting behind us.[24]

Brigadier General De Lisle who had ordered the charge of the 9th Lancers and 4th Dragoon Guards was in no doubt that it had been the right thing to do and that moreover it had saved a critical situation. In a report afterwards he noted:

> The charge was well-led and gallantly executed by all squadrons. The actual effect was marred by a wire fence. The moral effect was complete, the enemy did not advance beyond the fence for four hours and gave time for the 5th Division to retire.[25]

Before the day was out, more bravery would be shown by the 9th Lancers, when a party under the command of Captain Francis Grenfell came to the assistance of 119 Battery Royal Field Artillery, which having gallantly kept the heads of the enemy down for most of the day, now found itself closely pressed by three German batteries

An artist's impression of the charge at Audregnies, 24 August 1914. (Author's Collection)

and a machine gun. Grenfell had already been wounded by shrapnel, but a shot of Dutch Courage had revived him:

> It felt as if a whip had hit me in the leg and hand. I think an artery was affected, as the blood spurted out, and my observer, Steadman, and young Whitehead very kindly bound me up. We also had to put on a tourniquet, and referred to the Field Service Regulations to find out how it had to be put on. This would have amused you. Of course, we found out how to stop blood in every other part of one's body except one's hand, but eventually came upon this useful information. Things began to go round and round, and I luckily remembered that in the wallets of the horse I had borrowed I had noticed a flask.

> This proved to contain a bottle of the best old brandy, and my observer and I at once drank the lot. I now felt like Jack Johnson, instead of an old cripple.[26]

One section of guns was safely extracted but four remained to be withdrawn, and Grenfell, whose exploits earlier on 24 August would result in the award of the Victoria Cross, led his men up to the guns to help extract them. He wrote afterwards:

> It was our good fortune to be thrown by Providence (after a good hard fight which threw us into complete confusion) behind a railway embankment, near the 119th Battery. They were occasionally firing and then, I believe, stopped. The brave way the two officers there behaved, and the dignified way the guns, still challenging, remained there, filled me with an admiration which I know will last a lifetime. No English regiment could have stood by without saying 'Can we give you a hand?' Had the senior officer done so he would not have been an Englishman. What we did was forced on us by the splendid example of the Battery, which had been set them by their two officers.[27]

Later he continued his account with a description of the way in which he rallied his men by recounting their proud history and traditions:

> It was not a very nice job, I am bound to say, and I was relieved when it was finished. It meant leaving my regiment under the embankment and riding out alone through the guns, which were now out of action and being heavily shelled all the time, to some distance behind, where I found myself out of range of the shells. It was necessary to go back through the inferno as slowly

> as possible, so as to pretend to the men that there was no danger and that the shells were more noisy than effective.
>
> I reported to the Battery Commander that there was an exit; he then told me that the only way to save his guns was to man-handle them out to some cover. My experience a few minutes before filled me with confidence, so I ordered the regiment to dismount in front of their horses, and then called for volunteers. I reminded them that the 9th Lancers had saved the guns at Maiwand, and had gained the eternal friendship of the gunners by always standing by the guns in South Africa; and that we had great traditions to live up to, as the Colonel had reminded us before we started.
>
> Every single man and officer declared they were ready to go to what looked like certain destruction. We ran forward and started pushing the guns out. Providence intervened, for although this was carried out under a very heavy fire and the guns had to be slowly turned round before we could guide them, we accomplished our task. We pushed out one over dead gunners. I do not think we lost more than three or four men, though it required more than one journey to get everything out. It is on occasions like this that good discipline tells. The men were so wonderful and so steady that words fail me to say what I think of them, and how much is due to my Colonel for the high standard to which he had raised this magnificent regiment.[28]

The 9th Lancers are arguably the best documented cavalry regiment of the 1914 campaign, for another letter also describes these events, this time from Trooper Walter Charman:

> We spent the morning under a hail of whizzing shells, in holding back the enemy in order that our infantry

might withdraw. After we fed the horses we were ordered to mount and take shelter behind some cottages. The enemy's fire became more galling to our men, and we were told to prepare for action. There were eleven of the German guns on the outskirts of a wood a mile or so away. We could not see them, but they kept up an incessant fire. The A, B, and C Squadrons of the 9th Lancers joined up, the 18th Hussars and the 4th Dragoons being in support. I was in the C Squadron, and my officer was Captain F. O. Grenfell, and his twin brother, Captain R.N. Grenfell, was in command of B Squadron. Colonel Campbell said that the guns must be taken, and the bugle sounded the charge. Away we galloped, over several fields of corn, under a hail of shells and rifle fire. We could then see the gunners at work, and we became furious. We yelled and shouted, and frantically rode at them, all the time meeting a withering fire. The hissing and the scream of the shrapnel was terrific, but nothing could hold us back or check us. The rifle fire ceased. We must have ridden their infantry down.

We cleared everything in front of us, and dashed through the barbed-wire entanglements. When within one hundred yards of the guns the gunners ran for shelter in the wood. Those who did not get away were cut up. We put the guns out of action, and yelled like madmen. Then we were ordered to go back into the village. Away we raced through another hail of shells from guns on our left, and there was a neck-and-neck race with death. When we pulled rein there were only seventy-two live horses of the 400 odd who faced the guns as the bugle sounded the charge, and many of those had to be killed because they were badly wounded. We took shelter under the railway embankment for three-quarters of an hour, and shells

> from a distant hill were still bursting over our heads. Our own battery of five guns was gradually being silenced, and my leader, Captain Grenfell, shouted, 'We must save those guns or the 9th Lancers will be wiped out.'
>
> Our battery was being shelled, and the position looked hopeless. We were again racing away, but this time to save our own guns. We had to face heavy fire, but we saved our guns. There was only one gunner left, and he was about to fire his last shell when we rescued him and took the guns away. It was in this action that Captain F. O. Grenfell was wounded, and he was taken to the hospital, but would not remain there. He insisted on leaving, and as we withdrew from the village he led his squadron. The commander of the infantry division thanked us for what we had done, saying we had undoubtedly saved his men from being cut up. General French sent a letter of praise, which was read to the troops, who highly appreciated his action.[29]

Dalmeny House, the Edinburgh residence of the Earl of Rosebery, was generously placed at the disposal of the naval and military authorities for the treatment of wounded from France, and in October 1914 the first group arrived. A journalist from *The Scotsman* was present and interviewed some:

> Another case in point was that of a light-hearted young trooper of the 9th Lancers. The wild charge of that famous corps when they rode to the rescue of the guns at the Forest of Compiègne has been termed the modern Balaclava. Trooper [Albert] Bridger, a Brighton lad, took part in the charge. Across a shrapnel-swept space of about 400 yards and right up to the guns they galloped. 'It was great', the trooper remarked. 'It is impossible to describe

> the thing. We were like men possessed – madmen for the time being. Chums fell on every side as we galloped onwards, but we never noticed them. We saw nothing but the guns. The whole place was screaming, what with our own yells, the rush of the horses, and the awful fire of the Germans. It seemed a long time, but we got there at last, limbered up, and rode back. But only about half of us.'
>
> The trooper escaped without a scratch, 'but it was a miracle', as he himself said. With a touch of pride he pulled out of his pocket a carefully preserved sketch of 'the wild charge they made', which had appeared in one of the British illustrated journals, and which had been sent on to him from home. 'It was as bad as that, and worse,' he remarked. It was the trooper's fate, however, to escape seemingly certain death in this way; and a few days ago to be surprised, by a party of Germans while on patrol duty along with a companion, and fall wounded in two places, shot in the leg and in the arm.[30]

There is no doubt that this action, however futile in military terms, captured the imagination of the country at the time and numerous artists' impressions and accounts appeared in newspapers. It inspired recruiting posters as well as a story in the *Boy's Own* comic. Wounded 9th Lancers were feted where ever they were found and there was a justifiable sense of pride among the survivors. Trooper George Pritchard of the 9th Lancers, for example writing from Netley Hospital on 3 September to his mother in Lorne Street, Wrexham, told her:

> I got hit in the arm with a shell. What do you think of the charge of the 9th? It was worth getting hit for, but don't worry, [it] shall be all right. Seven of our officers got killed last Thursday, but Captain Grenfell got picked up the same time as me. He is going on fine.[31]

Another of these local heroes was Bandsman Edward Humby of St Leonards in Sussex, a stretcher bearer who despite his obvious modesty the district newspapers were determined to lionise. In one of his letters Humby wrote:

> I am still in the best of health despite the rumour which you must take no notice of; perhaps it will be in the papers that I was wounded on the 24th August, as I am told it was so reported. It was only a slight wound, and healed up in week. I never left the ranks, and got it dressed in a Belgian hospital; they were so good me, and wanted me to stay. They gave me a splendid feed, the best since I left England; the menu was soup, pork chop, and duff. You should have seen my ears working, but it was so amusing; I could not make them understand what I wanted to do after they had fixed me up. I had to do a bolt for it, otherwise they would have kept there. Of course, I had a bandage on, when we were on the march, and the things people brought to me – meat, wine, and all manner of good things. I quietly smiled, and put them in my grub bag, or passed them on.[32]

The evening after the action at Elouges, Arthur Osburn, the Medical Officer of the 4th Dragoon Guards, finally located his regimental headquarters with which he had lost contact. He had had a long and confusing day, and remembered:

> Of the five hundred men of the 4th Dragoon Guards only about seventy or eighty could be mustered. The 9th Lancers, we understood, had suffered almost as severely as we had, and the 18th Hussars had also lost a good number. Everything appeared to be in confusion. But our regimental Headquarters, with whom I should have been

BANDSMAN E. HUMBY,

"C" Squadron 9th Lancers, son of Mr. and Mrs. H. Humby, Maze Hill Home, St. Leonards, wounded in Captain Grenfell's historic charge, has now returned to the Regiment at the Front.

L69 Bandsman Edward Humby, 9th Lancers, wounded on 24 August 1914. (Author's Collection)

all day, had apparently taken no part in the wild mélee that was to be called a charge. Our Colonel, 'Dick' Mullens, with all his staff, was safe, including Solly Flood our second in command, Pat Fitzgerald, Denis Darley, signal officer and Oldrey, the adjutant. Our C.O. was calm, but that night he was indignant, sorely grieved, wondering who had ordered his squadrons into this disastrous affair? No one could say! He did not appear rattled, though nearly all his officers and three-quarters of his Regiment

> were missing. Only about seven or eight of our officers could be found that night, yet, including various attached interpreters and French officers, we had had thirty-two that morning.[33]

The same day, Maddick was involved in an equally confused though less well known action north of Angre, when the 5th Lancers together with the 4th Hussars galloped forward and took part in a dismounted action, inflicting casualties on the Germans but ultimately being forced to withdraw, the commanding officer Lieutenant Colonel Parker being seriously wounded in the process. One of the soldiers of the 5th, Trooper Harold Eyre, noted in his diary that:

> During this period we had a bad time and I got my first horse shot from under me. We had a bad smashing up all round and had to retire.[34]

Maddick was more expansive in his description of the day's events:

> Monday, August 24. – At 2.30 a.m. I find myself shaken and the words 'Orders, Sir', to say the regiment will turn out at 4a.m. Get up and go down to the Sergeant-Major and warn him. Give up all idea of any rest, so join Madame and her friends in coffee, and in my most persuasive manner and best French suggest an omelette, &c., would be agreeable before we start. My suggestion is taken by Madame and several of her friends, who rush off to make it. I do hope it won't be a case of 'too many cooks spoiling the omelette'. Madame's male companion, who remains, muttered, 'Mon Capitaine, encore un petit verre.' Sound fellows, the Belgians. With the omelette 'Jim' B. and the Interpreter arrive, so we fortify the inner man against future contingencies! Time to get off, so will

bid Madame farewell and thank her heartily for all her kindness and great hospitality. Assure her there is nothing to fear from the Germans, that she is perfectly safe.

We march out and join up with the Cavalry Division at Audregnies. Heavy fighting going on on our right. Message comes about midday that the 5th Infantry Division are being hard pressed, and that we, the Cavalry Division, are to go to their help. In doing so we bump into the head of another German column of infantry, so have to take them on dismounted. My squadron is sent to support the 5th Dragoon Guards, who are heavily engaged. Leave my horses under cover of a sunken road running up a hill. Take up a position along the road on the top of the hill and join up with the 5th Dragoon Guards on my left. Great battle going on all round. Germans advancing in columns, great targets. My lads really do great execution. Can see the effect through my glasses, but still they come on. Getting hot, and several men wounded.

Men seem really to be enjoying it, to judge by the conversations I hear around me as I move along the line. Ordered to retire and take up a new position in rear. Retire by troops extended to our horses; have a nasty open bit of ground to cross, and the firing is heavy. However, we get across all safely and get the wounded under cover. Sorry my signalling corporal is hit – a good fellow in every way – great loss to me. Go through the village of Angre to our next position; on arrival finding V. and two rear troops missing. Again ordered to retire to a fresh position to our right rear; on the way pick up the Colonel.

A woman at a cottage is handing out beer; stop and dismount and have a glass – awfully thirsty. Hand the Colonel a glass, and go on up the hill. Just reach the top when a hot fire is opened. Colonel stayed at the bottom

> to bring up another squadron. He and 'Poolie' are hit, the Colonel badly, 'Poolie' slightly. Unfortunately the woman who gave us the beer was killed as she was handing out beer to the men. Ordered to retire on Bessigne, where the division is 'rendez-vousing'.[35]

At least one officer of the 5th Lancers, Lieutenant the Honourable Ivan Hay was to be taken prisoner the following day, after having been detailed to observe the approach of the enemy, a German corps advanced into the gap between him and the Cavalry Division. After being given directions by a British patrol, he attempted to re-join his unit by hiding in a French farmer's cart, but was intercepted on the road as he approached Le Cateau.

Captain Herbert Maddick, 5th Lancers, who published his account of the early actions of 1914 as *A Cavalryman at the Front*. (Author's Collection)

It would be difficult to overstate the disjointed, fragmented nature of the fighting over the next two days, but the British cavalry did its best to cover the retirement of the other arms in the face of determined pressure from the Germans. The role of the cavalry now was to delay the enemy's advance at all costs; to prevent a frontal attack developing, in case the weary and footsore infantry, forced to halt their retreat, should be attacked or perhaps destroyed by enemy cavalry. At the same time they had to prevent British guns and transport from being cut off. But, most important of all, despite reduced numbers they sought to protect both flanks of the several divisions in retreat.

From flank to flank, from dawn almost to dawn, by great zigzags across an embattled front the British cavalry rode throughout that Retreat. From hour to hour through those long dusty blazing days of August they hung on till the last desperate minute, while the slow-moving infantry got clear, coming often unexpectedly into action against German cavalry and horse artillery, and then fighting against the demoralization of bolting back to take up fresh and hurriedly-chosen positions.

Chapter Two

The Great Retreat

At the Battle of Mons the BEF, though faced with overwhelming odds, had managed to give the Germans a bloody nose. At several points along the line through sheer firepower alone the advancing German columns had been checked. However, the situation became untenable once German troops had broken through the French forces to the south. Now they threatened to entirely envelope the BEF, and the words of Secretary of State for War Lord Kitchener must have been ringing in the ears of its commander Field Marshal Sir John French. He was to co-operate with the French in every possible way,

Artist R. Caton-Woodville's impression of exhausted cavalrymen during the Retreat. (Author's Collection)

but under no circumstances was he to allow the BEF to be destroyed. To retreat west was unwise, because as the great arm of the German war machine swung around it would inevitably cut them off. Instead they began to withdraw southwards towards Paris. As they did so, the cavalry provided the rearguard, its men moving from position to position, slowing down the German advance as much as possible before falling back again.

Not surprisingly these exertions took their toll on the men. With little rest and seldom enough to eat, men would often fall asleep in the saddle, travelling some distance before being woken by an officer or NCO. When halts were called, the welfare of the horses came first and these weary troopers ensured that they were fed, watered and rubbed down before attending to their own needs. Maddick continues his account of the retreat, and attributes the successful extraction of his regiment from the unfolding chaos to his brigade commander:

> August 25, Tuesday. – Awake at daybreak and send out patrols. No sign of the enemy. Where can their much-talked-about cavalry be? Surely after yesterday's retirement they ought to be worrying us. Can it be that their cavalry is a fraud? Our Cavalry Division moved towards Valenciennes and manoeuvred round it. Wherever we appeared we were shelled. To me a meaningless day, as did not know what our objective was, or what we were doing, except having a very fatiguing time for men and horses ... We retired on Le Cateau, which lies in a hollow surrounded on all sides by high ground – a perfect shell-trap.
>
> We retired through Le Cateau. What a sight! A pitch-dark night, raining, the street blocked with guns, ambulance wagons, transport, infantry, cavalry, all going different ways. We managed with great difficulty to thread our way through and get clear of the town. I never saw such confusion. Lucky for us the German cavalry

> did not push on with their much-talked-of dash! We went on another four miles to Cotillon, where we billeted (the whole regiment in a farm) and got our girths loosened and saddles off for the first time since 3 a.m. on Monday, and it is now about 10 p.m. Found that 'McBun' and the whole of A squadron, 'Henry' and one troop of C squadron are missing. Probably got cut off in our retreat by 2nd Cavalry Brigade, which was near us. Hope they are all safe. Two troops, 3rd Hussars, joined on to us. Cavalry Division seems rather mixed up. Perhaps we were nearly surrounded. Feeling in regiment is that General G. [Gough, commanding 3rd Cavalry Brigade] has saved us from a disaster.[36]

On 26 August came the anniversary of the Battle of Crécy, which took place in 1346. The weather that morning was hot and misty, much as it had been 568 years earlier. The similarities did not end there, for once again a small force found itself in a desperate situation, faced by a numerically superior and confident foe. The men of the BEF were now exhausted by the retreat, and though the original intention had been for them to continue to withdraw, Smith-Dorrien instead issued orders for them to stand their ground. As the two corps of the BEF had now lost contact with each other, the battle would be fought by II Corps alone, with a thin screen of cavalry in front attempting to cover the gap between to the two formations and to prevent the latter from being outflanked. Maddick writes in extraordinary terms of his admiration for the men under his command, indeed the degree of mutual respect between officers and men is an often underestimated factor when considering morale on the Western Front in the First World War:

> August 26, Wednesday. – Up and ready to move off at 4.30 a.m. Moved back to Le Cateau. Did not enter the actual town, but went round the high ground to the South

of it and took up a position on the W. of it. Great battle going on. Fifth Infantry Division having a bad time of it and retiring. We cover their retirement. My squadron on high ground overlooking a railway embankment about 2000 yards again. Our Infantry gradually retire through us. The Colonel of —— Regiment thanked me for our support; poor fellows, his regiment had been badly mauled. Heard 'McBun' with his squadron had been seen in Le Cateau early this morning, so they are safe. We retire in a westerly direction and manoeuvre on the flank of the 5th Infantry Division. Late in the afternoon we see in the distance a division of Uhlans. The General tells us he has decided to take them on, but we shall charge at the trot, as our horses are dead beat.

We, the 3rd Cavalry Brigade, manoeuvre and get the favourable ground, and the Uhlans, after having a look at us, refuse the fight we offer and disappear. Cowards! Fancy a division refusing to take on a brigade! Great disappointment among all ranks, as we are all longing for a cavalry fight. All this dismounted work against infantry in vastly superior numbers is most disheartening. We retire to ——, where we arrive about 11 p.m., and halt to water and feed the horses. Get some food. Everyone awfully tired – raining hard. The orders come that we are to march at 1 a.m. Explain to men we are in rather a tight place, and that in spite of their fatigue everyone must buck up. Men lie down on the pavements and hold their horses. What a sight! Men and horses absolutely exhausted, but yet there is that spirit of cheerfulness which never fails Tommy Atkins even under such conditions as these.

It is apparent to everyone that we have taken the 'knock': with most armies one would say beaten, but with Tommy Atkins you can't say that, as it would not be true,

> as the only way to defeat him is to kill him; otherwise he just goes on suffering every hardship without a grumble, and then, when you think he is absolutely done, he turns round and hits you. People at home don't realise and understand what heroes the men are. Brave, suffering every hardship without a grumble, loyal, and in the highest sense true, typical Britons. And yet there are people who dare to object to a soldier in uniform being allowed in the more expensive parts of theatres, &c. Good God! it makes me mad: such people are not fit to black Tommy Atkins' boots.[37]

Once again here, Maddick expresses the regular cavalry officer's disdain for dismounted fighting, and the preference for horse-against-horse combat as the true role for the arm. Maddick's words provide support for the idea that in spite of the hardships of the Retreat, and the confusion and weariness which resulted from it, these circumstances were not completely without advantage. The adversity – loss of personal kit, lack of sleep, and absence of spare clothes – had its use, for it served to harden a military machine that had grown soft in the years of peacetime soldiering. It threw officers and men together in a way not known since the turn of the twentieth century, and gave a new temper and edge to the soldiers who experienced it.

On 28 August another British cavalry charge took place, this time at Moy, carried out by the 12th Lancers. The whole of the 5th Brigade was concentrated here; patrols were out, while a whole squadron of the Greys commanded the approach of the entire valley in which the lancers and the nearby 20th Hussars were sheltered. The brigade was thus well safeguarded against any surprise. However, whilst the British cavalry were providing a screen against German attacks from the direction of St Quentin, a number of enemy horsemen penetrated a narrow wood. Perhaps imagining that the British force in front of them was rather weaker than it was, a strong squadron

1379 Trooper Charles King, Royal Horse Guards (The Blues) who was wounded and captured at Viesley in a skirmish during the Retreat from Mons on 28 August 1914. (Author's Collection)

suddenly burst over the brow of the hill, and dismounted well down the forward slope. They then opened fire from a standing position in front of their horses. These men now came under fire from J Battery Royal Horse Artillery, and from the machine guns and rifles of the 12th Lancers, scattering their horses. Some had already started to surrender even before the mounted lancers came into action. It was a testament to their discipline, and the effectiveness of their pre-war training that after having charged through the enemy, instead of scattering the lancers rallied, reformed and charged again. A member of this regiment who was present here was Private Bernard Flynn of Oswaldtwistle, Lancashire; like a number of other men in the regular army he served under a pseudonym, that of Cameron, because of the stigma still attached to military service in some quarters. He wrote home to his father about the events of that day, stating:

> Did you read in the papers how the 12th Lancers charged, and saved the situation? A grand go it was, and we didn't

> half splatter them. We have hard times here – two or three hours sleep every night. We haven't to give these German devils a chance; they are so treacherous … They are frightened to death of us getting at them with the lance. We charged them the other day, Friday. We were only about 500, and though there was a thousand of them they threw their arms on the ground and surrendered. That's the German army, they haven't got the heart of a flea … Mons was a terrible battle, and we haven't stopped the work since last Sunday, so we are amongst them alright … I enclose a cutting from a newspaper, but it is not correct. It was the 12th Lancers that did this charge, not the Scots Greys who did not come on the scene until it was over. They were not in the charge at all, only the C Squadron. They call us 'The Charging Squadron'.[38]

Some of the men had been washing themselves in a body of water when the incident occurred. One of the soldiers involved was Trooper Frank Field, whose letter home describing the incident was published in a local newspaper:

> … a squadron of ours charged in shirtsleeves. It was like this. We were having a wash at a stream, and suddenly one of our scouts came in and reported about 200 German cavalry, and, by riding along the ridge, we were enabled to dash through a gap and catch them by surprise. We got the order to form line and then the exciting moment of every British cavalryman came, the order to charge. We went through them twice, and I might remark there were very few left (Germans I mean). One officer we captured called us a 'howling lot of devils let loose from hell,' and I don't think he is far wrong – ours is a mad lot when they get away.[39]

Frenchman Paul Maze was attached to the Royal Scots Greys as an interpreter, and also witnessed the whole event; he recalled that many of the men were resting, lying in the hot sun, when at about 11.00 am a report came in from one of the outlying patrols that it had been driven in from its position, having been engaged by enemy scouts. Two German squadrons had been observed advancing a little way behind them. There was an immediate flurry of activity as Major Swetenham of the 12th Lancers galloped off with his trumpeter and the Greys' squadrons mounting and dispersing with a section of guns. Maze remained with the limbers of J Battery RHA, eager to see what happened next. After some time, the rest of the battery was ordered forward and he jumped on to a limber that was moving off. By a high bank, where the led horses of one of the troops had been left, they stopped.

At that moment rapid musketry fire opened from the top of the bank and, just as he reached the men, who were firing from behind a hedge at an advance guard, bullets whistled through the leaves. These were coming from halfway up the distant spur, where a large body of cavalry had dismounted, and over which J Battery's shells were now bursting. The next second the enemy's horses, which were being quickly led to shelter, were stampeding, scampering up the hill, caught in the rapid fire of the machine-guns of the Scots Greys.

> What followed was timed to perfection like an event at a tattoo, when, suddenly, from the corner of the ring, deployed cavalry appears and a charge finishes the tableau. J Battery lifting its fire, the 12th Lancers who had worked round the right of our troops unobserved, sprang on the scene at full gallop, dashing for the flank of the disorganised Germans. The charge went through them like a flash, and the men pulled up their horses, re-formed, and once again rode through the enemy. By the time that the Greys had come on ready to charge, the

work was done; only a confusion of dead and wounded was left on the ground.

I ran down into the valley as one does towards the scene of an accident. Remounted squadrons with drawn swords were also hurrying to the scene. As a few Germans were hiding in the corn-stooks, lances and swords were thrust through the hay and I heard fearful yells. The horses were very excited, as were the men, who were showing to each other blood dripping off their sword blades. Others were busy picking up souvenirs.

Meanwhile, I had propped up a wounded German Dragoon, who was vomiting quantities of undigested, unripe, gooseberries. He had nasty sword thrust through his chest. In broken English he told me that he had only left the Ritz in London twenty days before, where he had been a waiter, but what I was interested to find out was whether they were the vanguard of a large force of Cavalry. He said that several divisions were in the vicinity. I wrote this down on a piece of paper and had it immediately sent to the Colonel. By then, the regiments had re-formed and were drawing away from the scene, and as I could see myself being left behind again, I hurried towards where I had left the limbers. I was just in time, for they were off, and I was cursed by the sergeant for leaving them, as he said that an officer had instructed him to keep an eye on me.

At that moment our guns unexpectedly fired again. It was Captain Dendie who, just as his section was limbering up, saw another advance party of enemy Dragoons on the reverse slope. Taking advantage of a target with open sights, he ordered his guns to re-open fire. This opportune intervention gave the brigade time to withdraw at leisure. As from my limber I looked round,

> I saw Major Swetenham's trumpeter coming towards us, leading a horse with an empty saddle. I guessed at once what had happened – Major Swetenham had been killed. I felt his death deeply. He with another officer, who had been shot through the head, and six wounded men were our only casualties in that engagement.[40]

In three long columns, the Greys, Lancers and Hussars were now trotting across stubble fields in the wake of the brigade staff, who were riding ahead with their escort, identified by a red pennant

Captain J.C. Mitchell, 12th Lancers, who was killed in action whilst leading his squadron in a charge against German cavalry at Moy, during the Retreat from Mons, on 28 August 1914. (Author's Collection)

fluttering from a lance. With them rumbled the Royal Horse Artillery battery, whose wheels crushed a path through the straw. As so often happened, a stray dog that had suddenly appeared from nowhere, tagged alongside, delighted with his new attachment. A feeling of satisfaction ran through the ranks, and the horses trotted on proudly. There was good reason for this elation – the enemy horsemen had been dealt a blow which would make them realise that they still had to reckon with the British cavalry. It seemed incredible at the time that a large force of uhlans, with their reputation, should have moved over open country without throwing out strong patrols to reconnoitre the ground. (It would be wrong however to assume that they would not in future advance as they had done that morning, without taking the most basic precautions, because a similar incident would unfold at Néry just a few days later.)

This incident demonstrated an incidence of weak German frontal reconnaissance. No effort was made to discover the flanks of the British position or what lay behind, and the Germans had pressed on blindly, probably expecting to find demoralised troops, but instead came upon a fresh brigade of cavalry which up to that point had seen little action and which was eager to get at the enemy. The British by contrast acquitted themselves well in this action, Brigadier General Chetwode's reconnaissance screen was pushed well forward, and the troops were concealed to a high degree. Most importantly a large body of troops had been kept in reserve and was available when needed. The enemy had been caught off balance, and the British delivered a smashing counter-attack, but at the same time, whilst the enemy was still reeling the attacking force was quickly and skilfully withdrawn – the attack was not pressed too far.

The retreat was characterised by numerous small actions, in which sometimes individual squadrons sought to delay or impede the pursuing Germans. Again, there was a horse against horse clash when a squadron of the 3rd Hussars met German advance guards on 29 August, as the report of Major Clinch, the commander of C Squadron describes:

> The orders given to the squadron were to proceed towards Freniches to get touch with the enemy's forces reported advancing in strength on the Ham-Noyan road. The squadron proceeded to the village of Libermont, contact patrols under Lieutenants Whiston and the Hon. Donald Howard being pushed into the Bois de Hôpital on either side of the Libermont-Freniches road. Both patrols were heavily fired on and reported the wood strongly held by the enemy. The squadron, therefore, withdrew to the west side of the canal, and proceeded due south in the direction of Campagne. Lieutenant Whiston's patrol again crossed the canal on the Fretoy road, and proceeded towards Fretoy. The squadron in the meantime occupied a position holding the crossing on the Fretoy-Beaulieu road. Lieutenant Whiston's patrol dislodged a strong patrol of the enemy's cavalry from the village of Fretoy by charging them with the sword. Lieutenant Whiston then proceeded towards Freniches, but was quickly brought to a halt by heavy and continued rifle-fire. Lieutenant Howard's patrol in the meantime proceeded in the direction of Murancourt, but was soon halted for the same reason. The enemy was occupying the high ground in considerable strength. In the meantime a force of German cavalry, estimated at 500 strong, having crossed the canal near Libermont, occupied the high ground west of Cachy, thus intercepting the retreat of the squadron towards Cressy. Patrols were now withdrawn to the west side of the canal, and the squadron proceeded towards the crossing at Campagne, which was found to be strongly held by the enemy. The squadron then rode

> to Catigny where orders were received to withdraw and rejoin the brigade at Dives.[41]

Likewise, the official historian of the 18th Hussars wrote of the actions of this regiment on this same day; in their experience however the enemy cavalry were notably reluctant to engage:

> We rested at Plessis till 10am on the 29th, and busied ourselves in getting a supply of poultry, which we contemplated with much satisfaction and packed in a cart we had requisitioned, meaning to give every man a good meal later in the day. But the Germans thought otherwise, and interrupted us so forcibly at 10am that the cart and its contents took a hasty departure – and the wrong road.
>
> We had sent Lieut. Summers and 21 men of B Squadron early in the day to the village of Maille, about 4 miles to the north, to watch with other patrols the approaches from the Somme canal. Lieut. Summers soon had dealings with hostile patrols, drove them back, but bumped into a hostile cavalry regiment, came under machine-gun fire and lost three of his men. He sent back, however, some valuable information, and the Brigade was enabled to turn out and take up suitable positions astride the Ham-Noyon Road for delaying the enemy's advance.
>
> At first the regiment was placed in reserve at the cross-roads a quarter mile south west of Plessis, with the 4th Dragoons on the east and 9th Lancers on the west of the road, but it was very soon moved to the left of the 9th Lancers to prolong their line. The enemy was very cautious and the country flat and in places well wooded, so we only occasionally got glimpses of his cavalry, and then only of small bodies and of a particularly energetic officer on a white horse; but there was a considerable

> force in front of us and some field and machine-guns soon opened fire. We quite expected a cavalry action, but on this and many subsequent occasions, notably on the wide open stretches north of Compiègne, the enemy seemed to have no desire to put into practice those shock tactics, which so often had been the feature of his 'annual manoeuvres' in the past.[42]

The regiment now retired slowly, moving from one position to the next and halting, until by late afternoon on a shell-swept ridge they found themselves alone, all other British troops around them having withdrawn. They then made their escape galloping away under fire. Elsewhere other cavalry units were also providing a protective screen to retiring infantry and artillery. Corporal Charles Dorcas of the 16th Lancers wrote to his brother:

> It was a very trying time for men and horses on the retirement – it was marching and fighting night and day. We always caught the enemy's patrols 'groggy'. I had the pleasure of knocking more than one out of his saddle. We have all been very close to death on dozens of occasions, but by good leadership and luck we have come through it. I am certain that right up to the present time the regiment has had a charm over it.[43]

Arthur Osburn wrote in dramatic terms of the chaotic nature of the retreat – regiments broken up into troops or squadrons or even small bands, with no one really sure of the direction to take or where the rest of the regiment might be. Hordes of French refugees clogged the roads and made any sort of co-ordinated retirement an impossibility. Several times Osburn found his regimental headquarters, only for them to be driven out of the village or farmyard in which they were billeted and scattered once more. He made a highly prescient

5578 Trooper James W. Clark 16th Lancers. He arrived in France on 17 August 1914. (Author's Collection)

observation however, in that each time the 4th Dragoon Guards made a stand and looked likely to be overwhelmed by German cavalry, it was the Machine Gun Officer Lieutenant Fitzgerald and his guns that saved the situation. An unnamed soldier of the 11th Hussars wrote of his experiences as part of the rearguard:

> I was with Lieut. Drake when we were called upon to hold up the Germans (during the retreat from Mons). But what could a mere handful of chaps do against hundreds of their cavalry? But we would not give in. It was a game of hide and seek. We got separated in wood, and I did

> not see any of our fellows for ten days. I got rest where I could in the daytime and walked at night. At one place, a little village, I crept into a big wheat stack but it was nearly my death. The devils came into the village and said the poor people were hiding British soldiers. They then set the houses on fire, and I could see the flames coming my way. I managed to get out before the stack took fire, only to run into the arms of three of the Germans. They were as drunk as they could be, and I soon got out of their grips. If two of them are alive their mothers will not know them. But I was caught a little later by two more of them. I thought it was all over with me when one of them was shot dead by one of our chaps who was hiding. I didn't know he was there, and you may imagine my feelings when he came running to me. We got away, but we should have been riddled if they had been sober. I managed to find my way to Boulogne, and am now in hospital with a nasty gash in the shoulder and few minor wounds.[44]

Corporal L. Smith, a gymnastic instructor from the 12th Reserve Regiment of Cavalry at Aldershot was now serving with the 11th Hussars, and was involved in the same incident. His home was 16 Chestnut Row, Aberdeen, and he gave the *Aberdeen Evening Express* the following graphic account of his adventures following the fighting at Mons:

> The losses on both sides were terrible. Then started our long retirement. This, I may add, was like a dose of castor oil to our troops. We were sent right out in front of everybody to the 'place d'honneur', as my troop officer once remarked. After seven days of this hateful business, my squadron was detailed for rear-guard, our duty being

to drive Germans back whilst the remainder got away. On a railway cutting we were attacked by the Germans, who held both banks. Our lot got split up and I followed Mr. or rather Lieut Drake along with about 40 men. We tried to get across the country, but got caught in barbed wire, and the Germans then turned two Maxim guns on us. Here a lot of horses came down, but not many men.

We fought our way into a village called Houncourt, but found it seething with Germans and strongly barricaded. Before I reached the end of the first street my horse was shot in the belly. Seizing my rifle and in company with Lieut. Drake, we charged the barricades and made for a wood. Altogether eight men and one officer got away. We broke off in pairs, myself pairing off with Lieut. Drake. We spent three days and nights in the wood, with the Germans all round us. In fact we could hear them singing and speaking. Crawling on my stomach at night time, I dug some potatoes and turnips for the two of us, and on this we had to exist. Leaving the wood by night, pushed on to Cambrai, where heard the Anglais were. But on arrival found that they had left on the preceding day.

We hid in a wine cellar, but the Germans set fire to the house, and escaped through a ventilator. We crawled through the kitchen garden, and hid in wheat sheaves for the day. Moving south at night, where we heard firing going on, we averaged about 26 kilometres every night. By day we hid in hen-houses, outbuildings, and woods. I cannot praise the French people too much. They gave some food whenever they could, if the Germans had not been there before us. Near Avesnes-le-Comte we secured a motor car and drove towards St Pol, but before we got half-way we found a German

> piquet outside a house. The sentry fired three or four rounds at us as we raced past, but his shooting was rotten, and we got safely through the village. We went on to St Pol, and found the place still French. From there we trekked to Etaples, and on to Boulogne. On arrival there my officer interviewed the British Consul, and, in accordance with directions, conveyed through him, Lieut Drake returned to the War Office and I my reserve regiment at Aldershot.[45]

The officer, Lieutenant Frederick V. Drake of St Albans, gave his own account of these adventures in the British newspapers upon his return home:

The band of the 11th Hussars at Aldershot in 1914. Those with the rank of boy would be too young to proceed on active service, but many others in this group saw action in France later that year. (Author's Collection)

During the long retirement the odds were about twenty-five to one against you all the time. We were sent right out front of everybody to the 'place d'honneur' where we expected the French to join us, but they never came. After six days I was left with 36 men to hold the Germans back while the others got away; but we were surrounded by a brigade of German cavalry. First of all we tried get across country and were caught up in barbed wire, and they turned two machine guns on us. They killed a lot of horses, but not many men. We then fought our way on to the road which leads into the village of Houncourt. The village was held by the Germans, barricaded with machine guns, and as we went into the village, we were being shot at from behind and front, and there was barbed wire on both sides of the road. We galloped the barricade. I got my horse shot about 200 yards before I got to the barricade and was stunned a bit. When I got up again I found all the other fellows swarming on the barricade. I 'joined in the hunt,' and eight others, and I eventually got out of the village on foot into a wood, where I divided the men into twos and told them the direction in which to go and left them, telling each pair to hide in different parts of the wood.

We spent two days and two nights that wood, with the Germans absolutely around us; they were so near, in fact, that we could hear every word they said. The corporal, who was with me, poor chap, had a 'cigarette' cough, and I was in fear and trembling lest he should attract the attention of the Germans. Had he done so it would have been all over for us. Leaving the wood by night, we pushed to where we heard the English were – at Cambrai, but when got there we found they had left the day before. We then hid in a wine-cellar, and the Germans came and

> burnt down the house above us. We, however, escaped through a ventilator. We crawled out through the kitchen garden and hid in wheat-sheaves for the rest of that day, and at night we moved south, where we heard firing going on. We averaged every night about twenty-five kilometres. We always marched by compass, and always went absolutely plumb straight across country. Each day we hid in hen houses, outbuildings, or wherever we could, and marched by night. We found the inhabitants extremely nice. Wherever possible they gave us food – if the Germans had not taken it all.[46]

It was however considered bad form at this time to discuss one's exploits publicly in such a fashion, and Drake aroused the ire of a fellow officer, Lieutenant Colonel Archibald Home, formerly of the 11th Hussars and now GSO1 (general staff officer, grade one) of the Cavalry Division, who wrote in his diary:

> What a fool Fred Drake is to talk as he has done – the Regiment are furious with him. Why cannot people keep their tongues quiet? War is not a thing to buck [i.e. boast] about, one has only to see an attack to keep one quiet for a long time.[47]

This however was not the most extraordinary aspect of this story. One of the men of the 11th Hussars whom Drake had commanded was Trooper Patrick Fowler. He became separated from the rest of the group in the early stages and after riding about aimlessly, he abandoned his horse and hid himself in a wood near Bertry, where he spent the winter, living on whatever food he could find. He was eventually discovered by a sympathetic French family who hid him in a wardrobe for the next three years. German soldiers were even billeted in the house, but still he was not detected. Not until the final year of war did he emerge from hiding, only to be arrested by advancing British troops as a deserter.

Astonishingly, as he was being led away raving incoherently about his incarceration, a troop of cavalry passed down the road commanded by now Major Frederick Drake. Fowler broke away from his escort to speak to Drake, who recognised and remembered him. He was returned to the regiment and though offered leave, refused to take it. He was none the less too weak for active duty after his years of confinement, and was employed as an officers' mess servant.

A similar story was that of Claude Henry Bushell, who on 26 August became separated from the British forces near the village of Escaufort, just south of Le Cateau. Bushell, from Claro, North Yorkshire, was a Lieutenant in the Queen's Bays (2nd Dragoon Guards), under normal circumstances commanding Number 2 Troop, of C Squadron. That afternoon, whilst acting as a galloper, Bushell had ridden forward with orders for the 11th Hussars to fall back to St Quentin. After delivering these instructions to their headquarters, he advanced further to notify their patrols. In doing so, Bushell unwittingly passed through the lines and soon found himself surrounded by Germans. He was forced to release his horse and hide in a drain at the bottom of a railway embankment, where he remained for three days without food or water. As the Germans continued their pursuit of the BEF, their numbers thinned and, by the evening of 29 August, he was able to crawl out of his hiding place to make contact with villagers from Honnechy. They provided him with some food but, while he was eating, a peasant warned him that German soldiers were approaching, compelling Bushell to once again take cover among some nearby hedges.

While still in hiding, Bushell was informed by a villager that there were other concealed British soldiers. As an officer, Bushell felt it was his duty to take charge of these men. Wearing some borrowed civilian clothes over his uniform, he marched to their location and encountered Sergeant Taylor and ten men of the 11th Hussars, possibly some of the

Lieutenant Claude Henry Bushell, 2nd Dragoon Guards (Queen's Bays). Whilst riding forward at Le Cateau he found himself behind enemy lines. (Courtesy of the Museum of the Queen's Bays)

group originally under the command of Lieutenant Drake. They remained in a plantation for the next eight days, repeatedly eluding German patrols while being greatly aided by the local inhabitants, including the Mayor of Honnechy, who hid them, and fed them.

Bushell decided to relocate the group to an abandoned hut on the western edge of the Forêt de Mormal where other Allied soldiers soon joined them. The forest was large and densely wooded with heavy undergrowth, offering the soldiers an excellent hiding place. Bushell found himself in charge of thirty-five men representing several regiments, including the 11th Hussars, Royal Artillery, Manchester Regiment, Gordon Highlanders, Scots Greys, Munster Fusiliers, and the King's Own Scottish Borderers. There they remained for the next month, being fed by the locals while constantly under the threat of capture. Always on the move, and with autumn closing in, the party were aided at great risk by friendly Belgians. Eventually, Bushell was smuggled across the Dutch border and returned to the United Kingdom.

Another element of the British rearguard was provided by the North Irish Horse. This unit, along with its sister regiment, the South Irish Horse, had begun life during the Boer War as an Imperial Yeomanry formation. Both the regiments retained this status until the creation of the Territorial Force in 1908, into which Imperial Yeomanry and Volunteer units in Great Britain were absorbed. However, no

Territorial Force units were ever formed in Ireland and instead the two regiments became cavalry Special Reserve units. In 1914 both provided squadrons to support the regular regiments in France.

One typical story was that of Trooper Alfred Kyle who joined the North Irish Horse in 1913, and had undertaken camp training before mobilisation on the outbreak of war. As part of B Squadron, he went out with the first batch of 300 men, being conveyed directly from Dublin to Le Havre. There they remained for two days at a rest camp, after which they entrained for a point near the fighting line. At this time the Allies had retreated to the Cambrai-Chateau line. The North Irish Horse were instructed now to act as infantry scouts. When the Germans made their prolonged attack on the morning of the Le Cateau battle two troops of the North Irish Horse, numbering fifty-six men, of whom Trooper Kyle was one, under Lord Cole, were ordered to the thick of the fight.

Throughout the long and trying day they were engaged stemming back the German advance. The British outposts, he told reporters of the *Londonderry Sentinel* later, were taken completely by surprise, in as much as the German advance parties were attired in khaki and French uniforms. The British thought they were friends until they opened fire on them. This act of treachery, according to Kyle, so incensed the Allies that they fought with the greatest desperation, but still the outposts were almost annihilated. It was only the fine work of the British artillery that saved a few of these gallant fellows.

Asked his impressions of the battle, Trooper Kyle replied that after the first round of cannonading one did not seem to mind much what happened. In the rush and roar of the fight it was hard to think of details. Time after time the Germans were driven back with terrible slaughter, and at night the British lines were intact, but many sad sights were met with over the large battlefield. On the following morning, when for strategic reasons a further retreat commenced, the wounded Trooper Kyle was taken to a local hospital for treatment.

An artist's impression of the Battle of Néry, drawn by Philip Dadd from information supplied by a wounded man. Men of the Bays take five horses each to the rear, whilst the guns of L Battery RHA fire on the left. On the right, reinforcements arrive. (*The Sphere*)

Later on he was moved to a Brighton institution. He spoke in grateful terms of the great kindness of the French people to the British troops and the attention that was given to him when he was wounded.

The most famous minor action of the Retreat was probably the clash at Néry on 1 September 1914. Here the German 4th Cavalry Division under General Otto von Garnier, mainly due to heavy mist, managed initially to surprise a mixed British force of gunners and horsemen from the 1st Cavalry Brigade under Brigadier General Charles Briggs at rest in its bivouac area. Von Garnier on his own

initiative decided to attack the unprepared British force on horseback initially, but quickly changed his mind when the ground proved unsuitable and ordered his men to dismount and make the attack on foot; the Germans were eventually driven off with great loss. The artillery here comprised L Battery of the Royal Horse Artillery, whilst the cavalry included troops from the 2nd Dragoon Guards (Queen's Bays) and 5th Dragoon Guards. An officer of the 11th Hussars, which was also engaged, kept a diary which describes the action well:

> On August 31st, the 1st Cavalry Brigade arrived at Néry just before dark and billeted. At 4.15 a.m. on the morning of September 1st, a patrol, under Lieut. Tailby, was sent

out to the high ground to the north-east, and the regiment stood to arms at 4.30 a.m. The morning was misty, and it was difficult to distinguish objects at a distance of more than 150 yards. At 5.30 a.m., Lieut. Tailby galloped in carrying a German cloak, and reported that his patrol had ridden in the mist right up to a regiment of German cavalry on the ridge north-east of Néry, and had been chased back as far as the ravine …

Owing to the mist and a report that the French cavalry were coming up, fire was not opened on them until a dismounted patrol had been sent across the ravine to clear up the situation, and a good opportunity was thus lost. Meanwhile the enemy had been gradually working round to the south and occupied the sugar factory. ... Here they captured the owner and his workmen, whom they used when retiring as a screen against a party of the Bays under Lieut. de Crespigny. Several of the civilians were wounded, and the Germans escorting them made off toward their own guns. These unfortunate civilians took cover in a beet field until they were eventually rescued by us at the end of the action. At about 8 a.m. the 4th Cavalry Brigade arrived in support and opened a heavy artillery fire on the German guns. The enemy then tried to man-handle the guns out of action, but being under close range of the Bays' machine-guns (which were most admirably handled all through), and of the two machine-guns of the 11th Hussars, which had been brought round to the road at the south-east corner of the village, most of the enemy withdrew. Eight guns were left upon the field.

Our infantry now arrived from the North and passed through the village. C squadron were ordered to mount and follow up the German retreat. They crossed the ravine and worked round the left flank towards the German guns; Bell-

Irving's troop dismounted and opened fire on some thirty Germans who were retiring. Norrie's troop galloped through the German guns only to find them abandoned, and the advanced infantry closed upon them, the squadron pushed on to Varrines, capturing a number of prisoners and horses, and made good a farm about a quarter of a mile beyond that point; here they captured about thirty led horses and more prisoners. The squadron was recalled as the Brigade was ordered west. The whole action had lasted about two hours, during which the enemy kept up a heavy fire of guns and Maxims. The regiment kept up a heavy fire throughout, except during the short period as stated above.[48]

Above left: Lieutenant Colonel H.W. Wilberforce, who commanded the 2nd Dragoon Guards (Queen's Bays) at the Néry action. (Author's Collection)

Above right: 4328 Sergeant J.A. Fraser, 2nd Dragoon Guards (Queen's Bays) who was Mentioned in Dispatches for his part in the Néry action. (Author's Collection)

Trooper William Clarke served with the 2nd Dragoon Guards and was also present at the action at Néry. He wrote many years later of his memories of that misty morning, which were still remarkably vivid, adding that the fog had delayed the Bays from saddling up, and they were having breakfast when the first shells struck. He continued:

> I was one of a small party of about 15 men who were ordered forward to try to stop a German advance towards the sugar factory. The Germans had occupied some buildings alongside it. Lieutenants de Crespigny and Misa and a Sergeant Major led the attack. We managed to stem the Germans advancing for a time but due to casualties we had to withdraw. The Germans were machine gunning us from the sugar factory and I remember that the Germans were finally shelled out of the factory and outbuildings by 'I' Battery of the Royal Horse Artillery. Our casualties were heavy, Lieutenant de Crespigny was killed, and so were 2 or 3 other men and the rest were wounded. Lieutenant Misa, myself and one other man were the only ones to come back unwounded. I was incredibly lucky that day, and to this day, I can't remember how long we were actually engaged during our attack on the sugar factory.
>
> Then cavalry reinforcements arrived. They had come across our horses stampeding and they opened fire on the German guns … When the battle had ended, somewhere about 10am we helped to collect the wounded and cleared up, collecting bits and pieces of useful equipment. It was my first sight of multiple deaths in battle. Many men and horses, both German and British, dead and abandoned. At the count I think the Queen's Bays lost about 150 horses, at least half that amount killed, the others lost by stampeding. One officer and three or four men killed and

> perhaps 50 wounded. That's not counting men and horses of other regiments, such as 'L' Battery RHA, the heroes of the day. Everything seemed to happen so quickly, events were out of our control. I know that I felt frightened and excited at the same time. We were a very highly trained and efficient regiment, and we did as we were trained to do, responding quickly to a situation without question. And if you wanted to live you had to kill.[49]

Lost that day was the commanding officer of the 5th Dragoon Guards, Lieutenant Colonel George Ansell. A fellow officer, Charles Blackburne, wrote of him:

> Now about poor George; we were attacked at daybreak and the Germans nearly succeeded in stampeding our horses, we turned out dismounted close to the lines and held the Germans in check. T came up and, as I happened to be there, we had a word about the position (our left flank was unprotected). George told me to go there with what men I had. I collected a few. He then galloped back, mounted two squadrons, and went off with them, wide round the left flank. He rode up to the top of one ridge, ahead of his men, to reconnoitre, and they, the Germans, were close to him. They hit him and he rode back about fifty yards. Onc of thc last things hc said to his ordcrly was to go up into the firing line, as he would be of more use there. He was a brave man and I feel his loss most awfully. They got a doctor to him, but nothing could be done, shot through chest and back I am told.
>
> In my opinion the action George took in going round the flank not only saved the whole situation but established a panic among the Germans, who fled, and we captured eight of their guns.[50]

In the chaos of the retreat, men could be temporarily made prisoners and then liberated again in a matter of days, if not hours. One remarkable case was that of Lieutenant H.M. Hill of the 5th Dragoon Guards, who was also involved in the Néry action. One of his fellow officers wrote to Hill's sister on 4 September:

> Maurice was in my troop and I daresay you know three days ago we had a sharp skirmish with the Germans and my troop was heavily engaged in dismounted action against the enemy at about 300 yards. When the order came to retire we stopped to cover the retirement of another troop then retired again by sections – Maurice's section was the last to go. They lay down steadily firing while the other sections retired and when their turn came to go there was no covering fire from behind and I had to tell them to bolt for it. Of the section of 4 only one got out. Two were shot at once and Maurice wounded in the head within 10 yards of me and about 100 yards from safety. My troop sergeant returned about 2 hours later and got him into a farm where he is being well looked after.[51]

In fact, the sergeant had removed Hill's identity disc and when the farm was over run by the Germans, he was made prisoner. Still unconscious from his head wound, the Germans had no idea as to his identity. Later still, the farm fell back into allied hands, and Hill was taken to a hospital in Paris. He was still unable to tell the nuns who were nursing him who he was, and it was only some weeks later that his identity came to light, via a number on his hand-made boots. He never however made a full recovery, and later had a metal plate fitted to his skull. Hill died shortly after the war as a result of his wounds.

A remarkable and rare German account of the Néry action exists, in the form of a diary kept by a soldier who was present with the *Husaren-*

Regiment Königin Wilhelmena der Niederlande (Hannoversches) Nr. 15, a man named Gustav Ostendorf:

> From approximately at 10 o'clock in the evening, until 4am on the 1 September we were continuously on the march again, i.e., the only halts made were necessary ones to soak [the horses]. That made three days and nights [continuously advancing], fortunately in the meantime I had received an extra half loaf of bread from my Vizewachtmeister [sergeant] Hass. By this exhausting ride we had caught up with the enemy, who were occupying the village lying 2 km before us. Obviously they [the enemy soldiers] were also very tired, because for the time being everything remained calm in Néry, as the village was called.
>
> We attacked immediately, with our three cavalry brigades in an encircling movement, which meant that we came into the village from all sides at once, however we received heavy machine gun fire from the houses, which cost us heavy casualties. In order not to be overwhelmed by the English infantry, we had to pull back and we now proceeded in skirmish line [again into the attack]. Our guns had taken up the fight with the English artillery, which at the strength of three batteries came into action before the lime sandstone factory left of the village. We took cover in the oats field as our artillery roared, this artillery fire had already destroyed seven enemy field guns. One enemy gun [pulled by horses] came out at the gallop from the village, it had hardly been touched whilst at the factory, but then this also was hit by two shell bursts together. Thus we did not have much more trouble from hostile shells, however at the same time, our guns had been reduced just to four, partly by barrels exploding.

> Suddenly we heard the Englishmen shouting to the left of us; they were quickly halted [by artillery], but they had already taken prisoner 10 or 15 men from the left wing.
>
> On the following day, 2 September, we set off away from the enemy, since they possessed a substantial superiority over us. We tried throughout the day to escape, but we did not find a way out. The noose pulled ever more closely around us, who were then silently with man, horse, wagon and cannon waiting in the darkness of a forest, with thick undergrowth and mountains towering above. So complete was this cover, that all were protected by it. Field guns, machine guns, flags and banners were buried. In this serious situation we spent full 2 days and nights, until by [sending out a] lone patrol we succeeded in making contact with our own troops behind us. In time we were again ready for combat, but for the moment however we required a rest, because for 3 days there was nothing to ease the growling stomach. It was all the more pleasing that we received two days of peace, which were completely spent preparing horses and riders, so that they were again freshly strengthened for the coming days.[52]

The action on 1 September has provoked debate and controversy ever since. In one sense it revealed a worrying failure by the brigade concerned to provide an effective security screen, which allowed the Germans to come within 600 metres of their bivouac without being detected, and then open fire. In this regard the German military historian Maximilian von Poseck believed that the British cavalry had 'failed completely' in its operational duty. Yet from a tactical point of view, the battle at Néry demonstrated the superiority of the British cavalry over that of the Germans, in this instance at least. Their commander General von Garnier lacked imagination and appreciation of 'ground'. He was obstinately intent on making a

The aftermath of Néry. Troopers of the Queen's Bays with two German prisoners (in lighter uniforms). (Author's Collection)

frontal attack against a village defended by machine guns which formed a difficult obstacle, and against an unsurpassable slope from the Saint-Luce plateau and Feu Farm. To guarantee success the Germans should have combined wide mounted flanking movements to the north and south, with their frontal fire attacks. General Briggs, a far superior commander, who had fought in the South African War and knew how to make the most effective use both of firearms and of the ground, immediately realised that it was necessary to act on the flanks, and his actions in deploying the 5th Dragoon Guards and Queen's Bays succeeded in stopping the German attacks.

Success was also due in no small measure to the fierce resistance put up by L Battery, the 11th Hussars and Queen's Bays in the centre. The most striking aspect from a cavalry point of view however was the complete absence of German reconnoitring patrols. A well organised reconnaissance should have endeavoured to find and estimate the enemy's frontage, and also identified the weak points in his position. It would have found a gap of some 10 kilometres between Néry and Crépy-en-Valoise, and rather than persisting in futile frontal attacks with insufficient numbers, the Germans might profitably have used a flanking manoeuvre and thus completely surrounded and captured the British position.

From a strategic perspective, the wider outcome was that the German 4th Cavalry Division was driven off, having suffered heavy losses and in severe disarray. Its three brigades took two days to reform and regroup, and its formations were in no position to attack retreating British forces which passed quite close to them, due to shortage of ammunition, exhaustion of men and horses, and the fact

1810 Trooper Arthur E. Lunn (second right), 12th Lancers, taken prisoner at Maubeuge on 8 September 1914. It seems likely that he was part of a patrol under Lieutenant Moore, cut off during the retreat from Mons and surrounded by the Germans in the Foret de Mormal. (Author's Collection)

PoW postcard sent home by 1811 Trooper Charles Dixie, 12th Lancers, wounded and taken prisoner at Maubeuge on 8 September 1914. He was probably also part of Moore's patrol. (Author's Collection)

that it had left behind several machine guns and all the guns of its three batteries of horse artillery. Even more seriously, First Army commander von Kluck had been deprived of his reconnaissance arm at a critical moment. He was consequently not aware that new French forces were massing on his flank, and that the manoeuvre which would give the allies victory in the forthcoming Battle of the Marne was already in preparation.

Chapter Three

The Battles of the Marne and Aisne

As the retreating BEF had begun to arrive on the outskirts of Paris, its various formations were instructed to concentrate once more, south west of the village of Coulommières – the retreat had ended, but the leading elements found roads blocked with felled trees and shops shuttered in anticipation of the imminent arrival of enemy forces. The Germans however had made a colossal miscalculation. Instead of their forces passing to the north and west of Paris in order to encircle the city (as the original version of the Schlieffen Plan had decreed), the German commanders lost their nerve. Fearing that their supply lines were overstretched, they instead elected to pass on the eastern side of the city. German commander von Kluck veered south-eastwards, in an attempt to smash the French 5th Army, and his change in direction was noted by British airmen. In what became known as the 'Miracle of the Marne', the German armies had now thrust their heads into a giant sack.

Simultaneous attacks by the French armies to the east, and the garrison of Paris sallying forward from the west, forced the German First and Second Armies to divide to meet the twin threat. A gap opened between them, into which the BEF was to advance. This, together with the French counter-attack threatened to cut off and surround the Teutonic legions. The Germans, having reached the banks of the Petit Morin, were to find that the river marked the limit of their advance. In what became a panic-stricken rout, it was now the turn of the German army to withdraw in confusion. The British and French managed to push them back as far as the banks of the

River Aisne, but here resistance began to stiffen as the enemy dug in. They would continue to observe the allies from their carefully chosen positions on the high bluffs overlooking the river here almost until the last days of the war.

The morale of the British cavalry was still extremely high, in spite of the hardships of the Retreat. A soldier of the South Irish Horse, in the troop commanded by Lieutenant Francis Brooke, wrote to his family at home:

> It is a wonderful experience for us. We are no longer 'summer soldiers'. I feel quite satisfied on that score. When I think of myself at times – dead fagged out after a long day, making my poor old charger as comfortable as possible, then 'turning down' anywhere, sometimes on the roadway, to sleep, as well as if I was in my snug little feather bed at home; then no sooner warm and 'cushy', as they call it, we have the order to 'Saddle up' and 'turn out'. It is a great life. I feel more the hardened old veteran each day, and don't care a straw where they send us. I may not tell you where we are, but I am proud say we have seen as much sport as most of them. From time to time we have had some exciting moments. A couple of days ago while we were having rest we were shelled out of our 'Biver', but that's getting quite a usual thing nowadays with the enemy's long range guns. It is the finest thing in the world to watch our artillery work. You can imagine our aeroplane flying over the hiding enemy; then bringing back information of his position. At once the artillery get the range, and – 'good evening'.
>
> We are being looked after splendidly. Our officers are all kindness and consideration. The major is typical warrior, and thorough sport (as you well know). We don't care where he leads us, we are so fond him. We are fed

> like 'fighting cocks'. Plenty of bread, cheese, bacon, jam, tea and sugar (no milk, of course). I shall teach you all how to drink black tea next 'Black fast day.' At present we are having rest – pour ainsi dire – but we expect to move off any moment on a long journey. Our horses wanted the rest badly. They are in good condition again now.[53]

This regiment, like its counterpart the North Irish Horse, was a Special Reserve formation. Each regiment had sent one squadron only to France upon the outbreak of war, and they served as Army troops, outside of the brigade structure of the regular cavalry.

In the 4th Hussars, as in probably most other British cavalry regiments, the horses were now very tired and were suffering from worn-out shoes (this in spite of the fact that, at the start of the campaign, each man had carried two spare shoes in the shoe case on his saddle). It had proved impossible to replace these up to now, due to lack of spares but on 5 September the regiment met up with its echelons for the first time since 25 August. These supply wagons were a welcome sight as they contained a certain amount of spare kit, and the much-needed horse shoes. The regiment, though much depleted (a strength of 18 officers and 265 other ranks was recorded) was eager to resume the offensive, and on the night of 5 September a general

Lieutenant F. de V.B. Allfrey, 9th Lancers, killed in action on 6 September 1914. (Author's Collection)

advance was ordered for the following day. The terrain however was difficult country for horses; it was thickly wooded, with many German stragglers holding out among the trees. Although large columns of retreating German infantry could be seen in the distance, the river crossings in the valley bottoms were often strongly held by machine-gun teams that proved difficult to dislodge.

* * *

On the morning of 6 September the change in mood among the men of the BEF was palpable. For the first time since Mons they were advancing. For one of them, however the day had unfortunate consequences. Private Fred Heseltine of 51 Compton Crescent, Leeds, the *Yorkshire Evening News* reported, was a splendid specimen of the British lancer. Private Heseltine had joined the 12th (Prince of Wales') Royal Lancers in January 1912, and was sent to France with the 1st Cavalry Brigade at the outbreak of the war. He took the rough side of the day's work with perfect cheerfulness, but at that particular time he was suffering under a serious grievance. He was in all the fighting around Mons, took part in the whole of the rearguard actions that marked the retreat upon Paris, and came through all this without a scratch; but on the second day of the Battle of the Marne, when the Germans were giving way and the British were hoping to get some of their own back, Trooper Heseltine had the bad luck to be bowled over by a piece of shrapnel and was invalided home.

The main body of his regiment was dismounted in the firing line when Brigadier General Sir Philip Chetwode gave the order to cease firing, mount and retire. Heseltine was holding his section leader's horse, to enable him to mount, when a shell caught him in the back 'with a blow like a sledge hammer'[54] wounding his horse in three places at the same time. Fortunately, the horse was still able to gallop and his rider to hold on for the mile and a half to the nearest field ambulance. From there he was sent to St Nazaire and evacuated home. He was wounded on 6 September, reached England seven days later, and after spending three weeks in hospital at Cardiff was released to go home. The wound was a bad one, for a piece of jagged iron went in at his back, broke a rib, tore the base of the lung, and passed out through his chest, making an inch and a half hole in the course of its passage. The medical officers at Cardiff who X-rayed the wound, told him that if he had been sitting upright in the saddle instead of leaning over to assist his section leader to mount, he would have been killed outright.

The initial contacts on the ground during the Battle of the Marne were characterised by short sharp cavalry actions. The Germans were attempting to screen their withdrawal by using several regiments of mounted troops strung out along the Grand Morin River. This was largely unsuccessful, as all three army corps of the BEF were across the river by nightfall on 7 September. British cavalry led the advance, and Lieutenant Jock Crabbe of the 2nd Dragoons (Royal Scots Greys) in his memoir describes a typical encounter with the Germans. A troop from the regiment had already been ambushed at Rebais, and the survivors were pinned down in houses unable to make further progress. Crabbe was hastily ordered to go to their assistance. He writes:

> I gave orders [to the men] to hand their horses over to the horse holders and got ready to attack, and while this was being done my plan had to be framed. What was I to do? There was Rebais, its roofs just visible through the trees, on a rise about 600 yards distant, and in some houses somewhere on my right front were the remainder of the [other] troop unable to get on. Obviously my task seemed to be, not so much to take Rebais independently but to do so in conjunction with them. Then what was the best way to do it?[55]

Crabbe and his men charged headlong up a stream, with the tall nettles along the side and the tree canopy above making it seem increasingly like a tunnel as it narrowed towards the end. His plan brought them out into the main square, where the horses of the Germans were corralled. He told a party of men off to try to stampede them. The excitement and adrenaline of what happened next is palpable:

> Off I and my trumpeter dashed, he with a rifle and I with a revolver, through houses and back gardens, across a street, more gardens and through another house, until we came out in the corner of a second square just north of [that] where the horses were. I had just started to cross the square when there was a crack of a bullet past my head. I flung myself behind a front garden balustrade just as another hit it by my ear. There was I in the middle of a village for all I knew full of Germans, armed only with a revolver. I looked for the trumpeter, only to see him lying taking cover behind the corner of a house about 15 yards to my right but in such a position that he could not fire down the square. I shouted to him to fling me his rifle which he very skilfully did as it landed on the little piece of grass behind my balustrade. It is hard to say how thankful I was when I had that rifle safely in my hand as it gave me such a sense of confidence compared with that revolver. I peered slowly round the right side of my balustrade and at once spotted my friend taking cover behind a tree at the far end of the square. He had his rifle to his shoulder ready to fire when I gave him a sufficiently good target. But he just waited a fraction too long as I got in the first shot and he fell backwards into what looked like a ditch.[56]

Crabbe now decided to wait for events to take their turn:

> It could not have been more than a few seconds later when, to my great relief, rapid firing broke out on my right and I hoped my troop were shooting straight and being successful. Amidst the shooting I could hear shouts and the galloping of horses. A few mounted Germans crossed me going all out; I speeded them up unsuccessfully with some parting shots … I gave the trumpeter back his rifle and left him at the northern exit of the village to keep watch, while I went back to find out what my troop had done or were doing. When I got to the main square where the German horses had been, I found the bulk of my troop either rounding up some loose horses or being hugged by the local inhabitants who at the departure of the Germans had suddenly come out of their cellars and hiding places. There were a few dead horses lying about and a couple of wounded Germans of the 8th Dragoons, but to prove that they left in a panic 47 lances were picked up.[57]

On 7 September the 2nd Cavalry Brigade was acting as a flank guard with the 9th Lancers to the front. They engaged a squadron from one of the German Uhlan regiments, the 1st Guard Dragoon Regiment, in a 'lance against lance' action. An eye-witness to this clash was the American motor-car owner Fredrick Coleman, who was attached to brigade headquarters as a messenger. He recorded:

> Behind a friendly stone wall, I stopped and took out my glasses. The stubble stretched away towards a line of woods. Diagonally, across the broad road that led north from the village, came a line of horsemen. Magnificent in the morning sun they rode, a solid line rising and falling with regular cadence, as though mechanically propelled.

The 1st Garde Dragoner Regiment of Berlin, of the Garde Cavallerie Division of the Garde Corps, the proudest, finest cavalry of the German Army – over one hundred of them, seeming double the number to me – were charging across the fields. On they came, like machine-made waves on a machine-made ocean. Then from the left shot other horsemen, one well ahead, another not far back, and a scattered scurrying bunch of two score behind, riding like mad, full tilt at the ranks of German pride and might bearing down upon them.

Colonel David Campbell, of the 9th Lancers, close on his heels Captain Reynolds, his adjutant, and forty-five of his gallant regiment were charging more than double their number of the flower of the enemy's horse. The Germans quickened appreciably, and their lances waved downwards to the rest. Their pace was slow compared with the whirlwind rush of the smaller band. I was on the wall when the impact came. Crash! went the 9th into the Garde. Colonel Campbell and Captain Reynolds were down, and horses reared and staggered. I wondered that none of the chargers funked it. Each horse seemed imbued with the spirit of his rider. Not one charger 'refused'...

The 9th scored heavily off their more numerous foes. A few fell, but more than double the number of Germans bit the dust. Crack British troopers proved their undoubted superiority, man for man, by the number of German dead and wounded we found on the field. Galloping on, the 9th circled round the village and away to the rear. The Germans stopped, and many of them dismounted. One of them went coolly through the pockets of Reynolds, lying with an aluminium lance through his side. A farrier-sergeant lay dead near a pond at the village end. The Germans knocked in his head and tossed his body into the

> pool. All this happened in the twinkling of an eye. Some of the Garde penetrated the village street, but returned after a gallop down and back.[58]

Medical officer Arthur Osburn came upon the scene shortly afterwards:

> In a field just below, near Moncel, I saw something moving. Walking up to it I recognized the wounded man. Colonel David Campbell, commanding the 9th Lancers, lay sprawled out in a field of clover. Forty yards from his feet and downhill was a small copse, a hundred and fifty yards from his shoulder and uphill a narrow belt of woodland. He had, if I remember rightly, a revolver wound in his leg, a lance wound in his shoulder, and a sword wound in his arm. This field had been the scene of a fine charge, a half-squadron of the 9th Lancers had just charged through a squadron and a half of German cavalry, and the deep clover of the field concealed many wounded men and horses of both regiments.
>
> 'I am sorry to find you like this, sir,' I said, kneeling down to dress his wounds.
>
> 'Not at all, my boy! Not at all! I've just had the best quarter of an hour I've ever had in my life!'
>
> I bandaged 'David' up, and within a few weeks he was back again leading his Regiment. This caused no surprise amongst those who knew him. 'David', said one of his subalterns to me afterwards, 'will someday go down and chase Satan out of hell!'[59]

This example of traditional 'shock' tactics was however closely followed by an exhibition of more modern mounted warfare, when a dismounted squadron of the 18th Hussars came upon the scene and was charged by a closely-packed German unit of about seventy men. The Hussars opened rapid rifle fire and felled about half of the enemy cavalry before they reached the firing line. Those who did reach it and passed through were mostly picked off by the horse-holders some yards in the rear. It is doubtful if such a crushing defeat could have been inflicted if the Hussars had been mounted, but it was a curious thing that two incidents should have occurred in one morning which bore so directly on the ongoing debate over British cavalry tactics. Two fascinating first-hand accounts of the actions of the 18th Hussars on this day survive. The first, from Sergeant William Armitt, reads:

> On this day 'B' Squadron had orders to make a flanking attack on a farm which 'A' Squadron were taking on in front. I remember we were very weak in numbers at this time, as my troop was only 10 strong, including the troop officer. We dismounted for action under cover in some undergrowth, about 1000 yards from the farm, and advanced in extended order towards it. There was a lot of firing going on towards 'A' Squadron, when to our surprise someone shouted that a squadron was charging at us on our left. Of course our object in view, the farm, was forgotten, and our most gallant and resourceful leader, seeing his opportunity, gave orders to take up a position and open a rapid fire. The squadron leader of the German squadron did not seem to have noticed us at first, and I believe he intended charging in the direction of the led horses; moreover we had left a troop with the latter, which no doubt led him further to suppose we were all in that direction.
>
> Their squadron, which was about 70 strong, was led to destruction by a most brave and gallant leader, for though he quickly grasped the fact that his men were in a hopeless position, he never the less changed his direction and charged down on our ranks.

As soon as we heard that noise, which sounded quite familiar to us all, we at once opened fire. After the first two rounds were fired half their squadron had fallen in front of a small railway line, and though the remainder pressed on, yet in an incredibly short time the whole squadron was wiped out. I say 'wiped out' because I know for certain that only three men got away, and I am sure they must have been hit several times as when they disappeared over the skyline; they had no lances and their horses were lame.

Immediately afterwards we advanced and occupied the railway line which lay just in front, from behind which the enemy had appeared. When we arrived there the sights I saw I shall never forget, as my position was right in the centre of the prostrate German line.[60]

Armitt dressed the wounds of a badly injured German officer, and gave him some of his water; the officer gave him his revolver and field glasses in thanks. The second account comes from Private Norton also of B Squadron:

> we could see no Germans so we lay down behind a railway about 500 yards to our front. No sooner had we done so than we saw a squadron of Dragoons charging at us, and it seemed to me they were making for the led horses. If they were they got more than they bargained for, as Major Leveson gave us an order to take what cover we could, behind the corn stooks, and open fire. We started firing steadily and the Germans fell from their saddles. I only saw three of them get away, and those must have accounted themselves very lucky, as the marksmanship of our squadron was excellent. We did our best for the wounded with water-bottles and bandages. We did not at first know what damage our fire had done,

> but found out afterwards that the Germans had 38 dead and 25 wounded. We had no one hit, I'm pleased to say, but two of our horses were slightly wounded.[61]

By contrast Osburn remembered that as well as Campbell there were numerous German wounded lying amid the clover where he was working, but in order to stiffen their morale, as raw recruits these particular men must have been fed lurid horror stories about the cruelty which would be inflicted on them if they were captured; as a consequence they continued firing at any British soldier that they could see, killing several. The net result was a vicious circle of brutality, in that the British were forced to kill any German wounded who did not obviously and immediately surrender.

There were many instances of brutality on both sides during the campaign of 1914, and often little evidence of the camaraderie between opposing front line soldiers which was supposedly a feature of the First World War. Prisoners of War fared particularly badly in many cases. However, there were occasional instances of humanity between enemies. Writing to his regimental journal in 1934, Major E.D. Martin stated:

> Lieut Baron von Bischoffshausen of the Jager battalion was wounded in the advance of the 5th Dragoon Guards at Sablonnières on the Petit Morin on the 8th September 1914. We were both wounded very near each other; perhaps he got me – I certainly did not get him as I was hit before I really saw anything. We spent that day in an ambulance together, then two days in a train to St Nazaire, and two more on the Carisbrooke Castle coming home to Southampton. There our ways parted. He asked me to try to get word home to his mother through the Chilean Embassy. As his brother had already been killed, he knew she would be in great anxiety about himself as missing.

> I did my best but am afraid without success… I feared that he might have died or lost his leg – he had a terrible wound in the thigh, which went gangrenous on the boat.[62]

That year of 1934, Martin had obtained von Bischoffshausen's address in Berlin and wrote to him. The German officer replied:

> I was more than pleased to receive your letter. Not only do I remember, but I have always to my mind the circumstances of our meeting and your comradeship and kindness in looking after me.
>
> Sablonnières, field hospital, transport etc are as fresh to me, and I can scarcely realise that twenty years have

Captain John Norwood VC, 5th Dragoon Guards, killed in action at Sablonniers on the Marne on 8 September 1914. He had been awarded the VC for an act of bravery in the Boer War. (Author's Collection)

> passed … I still have in my possession your card with the annotation '5th Dragoon Guards' … I have saved my leg thanks to the masterly and perfect care of the Chirurge, Dr Maloney, in Netley Hospital.[63]

Of course, the fact that the two individuals involved in this incident were both officers and from a higher social caste made a great deal of difference to their circumstances; and men from a lower class could perhaps expect rather less understanding and compassion if they fell into enemy hands. Another cavalryman who was captured by the enemy on the Marne was Private Charles Baker of the 20th Hussars. He recounted how, having been wounded near La Fère, he had been taken to a cottage which was being used as a temporary hospital. In there were about twenty wounded including three Germans. In the ebb and flow of fighting the British withdrew, leaving a party of German soldiers to find it. He continues:

> They were all more or less under the influence of drink, and they demanded that we should tell them where our regiment was. Not one of us would give the game away, and they thereupon said they would shoot us all. They commenced flourishing their revolvers and shouting, and I can tell you that I began to shake. I was really afraid then, and I thought our numbers were up. But the unexpected happened. The three wounded Germans implored their comrades to spare us, pointing out that they had been most kindly treated by the English doctor. That saved our lives. The next day we were removed to another hospital in a town, but as the Germans bombarded the place, we were again shifted. Even this move did not take us out of the danger zone, but ultimately we were taken to a place where we were absolutely safe.[64]

Lieutenant Jock Crabbe, of the Royal Scots Greys, who took part in a dismounted action at Gandelu on 10 September 1914. (Courtesy of Colin Crabbe)

At dawn on 10 September it was misty, and cavalry patrols from the Scots Greys reported large bodies of Germans near the village of Gandelu, apparently in bivouacs and unprepared to defend themselves. More than an hour was lost as in the mist conflicting reports mistakenly identified the body of men as French. Eventually an advance on the village was ordered but by then most of the Germans had left, with just a rearguard remaining behind and a column of wagons tantalisingly visible upon the horizon! Lieutenant Jock Crabbe takes up the story, describing another dismounted action, full of the chaos and confusion inherent in house-to-house fighting. The plan was for his troop to rush the village, before the Germans had time to react:

> Off we all started together in line, and once over the top the pace increased to a mad race as it was far steeper than we expected; our legs completely ran away with us and we were over the wall and into the garden before we realised how far we had come. I believe the Germans fired at us the whole way down and also at point blank

range in the garden, but though several tripped up falling head over heels, we all reached the houses in safety.

As soon as we emerged into the street I quickly realised that we were being fired upon from all sides, and as there was no place to hide, I shouted to carry on through the other houses and out into the wood beyond, where I knew we would be both under cover and have the village surrounded. We got there alright, and as now we were being sniped from both the village and the woods, I ordered one section of 5 men to watch the village and prevent the defenders retiring, while with the remainder I turned about and having extended to about 10 paces between each, we beat the wood as if for rabbits. Nearly all the Germans encountered were stragglers and had little fight left. Some were, however, foolish enough to have a last despairing shot and then hold up their hands imagining they would be taken prisoner. We had some quite good shooting at extremely close range though I did not feel bloodthirsty myself enough to fire at such poor game, and cleared the wood as far as the river.

On reaching it, thinking it was only a foot or so deep, I plunged in, but was completely taken in by the mud as it took me to the armpits. Just as I was clambering up the far bank, two Germans appeared from out of the undergrowth; so seizing my rifle by the muzzle I rushed at them and they threw down their rifles and fell on their knees.

[Now] we recrossed the river and went back to collect the section at Gandelu. When I reached them I noticed a white flag waved from a window, so boldly walking up to the village, Germans there began to come out of every house and fall in on the street. There were 39 in all, and when I was close to them the officer called them to

> attention and told them, what sounded like a few home truths in German. Then he turned to me and after saluting, drew his sword from its scabbard, and holding it by the point handed it to me in the old fashioned manner. At the same time he said in excellent English, 'These men are pigs; you should never have got down that hill; but most of them hid in the cellars; but you will not find the whole German Army like them.' I felt quite embarrassed as I did not know whether I was expected to say something in return and besides I was hardly looking my best, wet and muddy all over. But I merely told him to tell his men to lay down their arms on the ground and when my men had picked them up, we all marched back up the hill together to where I had left my horses.
>
> With the exception of that mad rush down the hill, when one had no time to be afraid, the whole fight was a picnic, as nearly all the Germans met were either so footsore that they were reconciled at being captured or they were completely lost in the woods. Again, we were lucky as we had no casualties, while in addition to the officer and 39 men captured, we had accounted for about 25 in the wood one way or another.[65]

Crabbe narrowly averted another friendly fire incident, when the gunners again mistook retiring British troops for advancing Germans, and he was able to warn them of the error. He continued:

> The whole fighting for the ridge had now become very scattered and no further progress was made until the Cornwalls, who had crossed the river east of Gandelu, made an attack from that quarter, and with their help the ridge was cleared. Then orders for a further advance were given … Much as I had enjoyed watching the battle from

> a safe place, I was very pleased at the thought of getting back to the squadron as I could not help feeling I was missing something. So we did not waste time; however crossing over the river I took the very sound precaution of making my troop throw all the captured revolvers etc. into the river, and along with them went the presentation sword. Not only did the collection of souvenirs add weight on the horse, but it was a certainty that one of these revolvers would go off in inexperienced hands and hurt someone … we took things peacefully only moving a further 5 miles forward to Passy-en-Valois. Now the very hot weather which we had had for the last fortnight broke, and we were deluged by a pitiless thunderstorm. As I was already wet from my effort in the river it made little difference to me, but we all welcomed it as we were fed up with the dust and heat.[66]

Among those wounded near here was a soldier from the Isle of Man, Sergeant Charles Christian, of the 5th Dragoon Guards. He regarded his experiences of the war up to that point (which had included taking part in a bayonet charge and having his horse shot from under him) as fascinating rather more than enjoyable, and wrote of the incident on 12 September which occurred whilst clearing Germans from a farm yard:

> I was shot down through both legs, and since that moment it has been my fate to see some of the worst sides of the war. I lay in a ditch for an hour with rain falling until the fight finished … After the fight we were taken in hand by the RAMC [Royal Army Medical Corps] and after our wounds were dressed we were carried to an improvised hospital in a church. I was hit in the left calf and right ankle. The calf wound was a nice clean hole, and it is nearly healed, but that in the ankle is more serious.[67]

2953 Sergeant Charles Christian of the 5th Dragoon Guards, who was wounded in September 1914. (Courtesy of Voirrey Johnson)

He went on to describe how the doctors' struggle to save his foot from amputation had not been helped by delays and difficulties in getting the wounded away by train.

* * *

On 13 September the British cavalry in France underwent a major re-organisation, with the original Cavalry Division being split up; the 1st and 2nd brigades now formed the 1st Cavalry Division. At the same time came the creation of the 2nd Cavalry Division, consisting of the 3rd, 4th and 5th Cavalry brigades under Brigadier General Sir Hubert Gough, formerly in command of 3rd Cavalry Brigade.

The two divisions now formed the Cavalry Corps under General Sir Edmund Allenby. The following day the 5th Cavalry Brigade crossed the Aisne via the bridge at Vailly, and came under intense German fire of all calibres. The hillside beyond was soon dotted with the dead grey horses of the 2nd Dragoons, and the attempt was abandoned. Crossings at other points were more successful however, and under cover of fog the BEF managed to gain a foothold on the far bank at Boug and Venizel. As the first files of the 12th Lancers topped the ridge above Gandelu on the morning of 16 September they saw:

> a truly wonderful sight – the little village below full of Germans, and many more of them streaming away through the woods ... and making desperate efforts to get a large convoy out of the valley.[68]

It was a cavalryman's dream. While the guns held up the convoy and the Greys cleared the village on foot, what happened next is recounted in the diary of Major Charrington. Major Crawley, commanding the 12th in the absence of Lieutenant Colonel Wormald,

> pushed the Regiment slap through the village, then away to the right up the hill; when we reached the top we turned left, formed line and swept along the top of the ridge, which was covered with retreating German infantry ... We captured over 200 and several machine-guns; also a Standard which, unfortunately, the R.S.M. placed against a haystack, continued the pursuit and was unable to find again when he returned for it later in the day ... Very few Germans were actually stuck, as they practically all knelt down and put their hands up, but a few of the rear files misconstrued the C.O.'s order to spare them as being spear them – and acted accordingly.[69]

While the Regiment was re-forming on the top of the ridge Crawley pushed forward 'B' Squadron to cover his left front, sending Lieutenant Wernher into Chezy where, with his usual aptitude for the bizarre, he rounded a corner with three men and found himself confronted by about 300 German infantry. Their astonishment was even greater than his own. Modestly he remarked:

> Being very weak in men, I discharged my revolver on them and galloped for it.[70]

The Germans were apparently so demoralized by this apparition that they were later mopped up by the infantry without a shot being fired. Crawley, meanwhile, considering that the regiment was extremely isolated, that there were no signs of the remainder of the brigade coming up in support, and that he was unduly encumbered with prisoners, determined to withdraw, ordering 'B' Squadron to conform and at the same time to cover his left flank which was very much in the air. Ironically it was now, after the battle was over, and from British rifles that the 12th Lancers suffered most heavily. For the Greys, seeing a mass of field-grey coming towards them and failing to distinguish the khaki of the escort, misinterpreted the movement as an enemy counter-attack. They opened fire on the 12th Lancers and their prisoners with a heavy and accurate fire, inflicting more casualties than had been received in combat with the enemy, though even then the total losses were only five men killed, two officers and eight men wounded.

The pursuit of the retreating Germans ended on the steep bluffs above the River Aisne, when they began to dig in and the first trenches appeared. Trooper Arthur Moore, of A Squadron, 12th Royal Lancers, part of the 5th Cavalry Brigade of the Expeditionary Force was a former member of the Lancashire County Constabulary, now serving as a reservist at the front. In a letter to a friend at home in Preston he described the action on 14 September when the regiment crossed the

Aisne at Vailly to support two infantry brigades, but after a day of intense shelling were forced to withdraw:

> My horse was shot by Uhlans at distance of 100 yards but I managed to escape after running two miles over mangle wurzels and rough country. How's that for reducing fat? I lost my cloak and blanket, which were strapped to the saddle. We have been under heavy shell fire. At one place we crossed a river by pontoon bridge, the Germans having blown up the road bridge. After we entered the village over the river we were shelled terribly. One shell dropped through the roof of a house – ten yards from me – and exploded. There were horses nearer to it than I was, and they were covered with plaster and fluff from the bedroom, which was blown through the window.
>
> We were fixed in the village, couldn't get out, with the enemy shelling like hell. We eventually retired back over the pontoon bridge, of which the German artillery had got the range, and shells were exploding all around it. I got through all right. My horse was grazed in two places, but kept on galloping. I think the horses are getting the worst of it. I have had three – two wounded and one killed. I have seen the result of our artillery fire. After a battle I went over the ground the enemy had occupied. There were many dead and wounded. The sight was terrible. We captured some prisoners at the same time.[71]

The discipline of the regiment in withdrawing in good order without panic or confusion was noted. On this occasion they were not needed in the trenches, but as the battle unfolded, dismounted cavalry would increasingly be used to support the infantry. At first the trenches

An artist's impression of British cavalry under shellfire in a French village, September 1914. (*The Sphere*)

were mere foxholes, as Ben Clouting of the 4th Dragoon Guards remembered:

> Our scoops in the ground, in which we lay, were in a sense the forerunners of the trenches. They were hastily dug by loosening the earth with small picks, which were then turned around to become shovels, the shovels being used to heap the earth in front, giving us a little more protection from bullets.
>
> We were to fight a sharp action from scoops when, a couple of days later, two squadrons were sent into action to support some hard-pressed infantry. Our orders, as I recall, were to ride to a ridge and open fire on the Germans reportedly advancing in mass formation on the far side.
>
> As a horse holder, I ought to have stayed behind, but older troopers were quite happy to let the likes of me go instead. Leaving our horses at the bottom of a ridge, we ran up the slope, where we dropped into small scoops made by some recently departed infantry. It was such a beautiful clear day as the Germans came on, packed together, hundreds of them, marching four deep and at a distance of some eleven hundred yards. They were coming down the far slope of a valley, marching through agricultural fields, as we opened up with our fifteen-rounds-a-minute-fire. The vision was perfect. I could see Germans toppling over as the rest came relentlessly on, but, with our artillery pounding away, the Germans could only take so much. All of a sudden they turned and bolted back up the valley, and the ceasefire was ordered; the action hadn't lasted much more than five minutes. We waited in those scoops until the evening, during which time a message was passed along from man to man. It came in an empty Bully Beef can and was tossed from scoop to scoop. It said, 'Brave A and C Squadrons 4th Dragoon Guards. You are a credit to both infantry and cavalry.'[72]

Men of the 4th Dragoon Guards, in 1914. Kneeling second from left is 8292 Trooper Ben Clouting, who took part in the charge on 24 August, and fought on foot on the Aisne. (Courtesy of Patrick Gariepy)

Such was the intensity of this fight that when Clouting went to replenish his ammunition pouches from the limber afterwards, he discovered that he had only fourteen rounds left of the ninety he had gone into action with.

That day, and for eighteen days afterwards, dismounted cavalrymen without either bayonets or entrenching tools were continually being rushed up to retake trenches, from which British and Algerian infantry had been driven out. It was not that cavalry were necessarily so much braver or more efficient, but because in such a hilly and wooded district cavalry could arrive practically on horseback in the firing line, fresh and unfatigued, after having been comfortably billeted all night in a village 4 miles away, whereas the wretched infantryman, already jaded with his marching, had no choice but to lie down in the mud on the spot and try to get what sleep he could in the drenching

Lieutenant Colin Barclay Leechman, 3rd Hussars, killed in action on 24 September 1914. He was initially reported missing but six months later, information from German soldiers indicated that he had been found dead in No Man's Land. (Author's Collection)

rain. Usually every evening the cavalry left the line, because their horses needed watering and cover from the rain. So for their sakes the troopers would ride miles back to dry beds, comfortable and safe, to the envy of the infantryman.

When out of the line, the men and horses were billeted in sleepy villages such as that occupied by the 9th Lancers, Longueval on the Aisne. Superficially they were tranquil, but this sense of security rapidly proved to be illusory when the Germans brought into action heavy artillery for the first time. These big guns had great range, and unlike the lighter 77mm shrapnel shells which had burst over them up to now, they fired lethal high explosive rounds. Sergeant William Martin of the 16th Lancers wrote to his father, a recruiting officer at Sudbury, to update him as to the latest happenings and in his letter he describes the effect of one of these large calibre shells:

> Considering the condition of affairs our men on the whole are looking very well ... The battle at the present time is raging furiously, and at any moment a shell might burst amongst us, but to tell you the truth we are so used to shells bursting now that we pay very little regard to them. Two days ago, our troop, consisting of 28 men, was billeted in a farmyard. We were trying our best to make up a bit of a dinner by collecting potatoes, carrots etc when a shell struck the roof of the building and set it on fire. Fortunately the only casualty was a wounded horse, although several of the men got shaken up a bit. The only thing that worried us was that we lost our dinners, because I can tell you we had to get out of it quickly – it was a bit too warm for Tommy Atkins. The country here is thick with woods, which makes it very dangerous for cavalrymen. We are fighting side by side with the French troops, and we get on very well together. Lots of them speak good English.[73]

A far worse disaster struck the 9th Lancers on 29 September as they were receiving their first substantial reinforcement since arriving in France, some ninety men and horses were parading for duty in a square paved yard surrounded by buildings and high walls, the former with fresh uniforms, the latter with gleaming saddles and other furniture. Osburn describes the horror which unfolded next:

> I was standing just the other side of one of the walls, with a letter in my hand, about to drop it into the Brigade post-bag, when down the wind from the side of the village which looked towards the heights on the further side of the Aisne came a low moaning sound, ominous to anyone familiar with the sound of long-distance artillery fire. The moan narrowed to a whining scream. There was a flash, a terrific metallic detonation, the walls of the building shook, and the air was full of dust.
>
> Fragments of stone, manure, pieces of clothing and hair came falling all about me as I ran through an archway into the yard and beheld one of the most heartrending sights I have ever seen, even in war. The detachment of the 9th Lancers had almost completely disappeared.[74]

In a scene of almost indescribable carnage, those closest to the blast had been killed outright and lay in a mangled pile of horses and men perhaps 5 feet high. Less lucky were those who now lay scattered around the edges of the yard. Osburn worked ceaselessly for the next hour to treat those who might live and to dull the final agonies of those who would not. Officers and men alike rushed to help, carrying casualties away to houses for treatment on stretchers, doors or other improvised hurdles.

But fate had a cruel trick in store. Later that afternoon the low moaning sounds were again heard in the skies above the village, and heavy shells began to fall once again. One, a dud, partially buried itself in the gutter of a narrow street. By ill-luck it had fallen outside a house used as a mess by the non-commissioned officers of the regiment, and several had gathered around it to look, for at this stage in the war dud shells – especially 8-inch examples such as this – were still something unusual. Osburn recalled:

> There must have been six or seven sergeants – one, a very tall man – and perhaps thirty or forty men there when I left. They were very pleased that this one was a dud. They were laughing and chaffing one another now; for the thud of its descent, after that morning's grim disaster, had caused many of them to bolt into safety.
>
> They did not apparently hear another whining moaning noise coming down the wind. I did, though I was then about two hundred yards up the winding village street. A terrific double report shook the whole village. ... For a moment I stood wondering where this last one had gone. Then breathless figures came dashing up the street towards me. 'Come quickly, sir! It's another one! It's burst and killed all the sergeants!'
>
> Running back with them, the morning's wail of agonized cries and shouts broke again on my ears. Though there was this time no moving mound of dead men, the sight was almost a repetition of what I had seen as I had dashed into the courtyard about six hours earlier. Evidently the unexpected, as usual, had happened. The second shell had landed on top of or alongside the first, and both had exploded amongst the group of men in that narrow paved street and between those high walls.[75]

As the war progressed the British would learn to avoid presenting easy targets to the Germans, and men would be discouraged from gathering in large groups when under enemy observation. At this

3793 Squadron Quartermaster Sergeant Leonard Finch, 9th Lancers, who was severely wounded on 29 September 1914 at Longueval. He died in hospital just over two weeks later. (Author's Collection)

juncture however most soldiers of the BEF held the Germans and their shooting in contempt. Trooper Thomas McCausland, North Irish Horse, a native of Ganvaughan near Castlederg, had been in France since 20 August, and had already taken part in the Battle of Le Cateau, where the rapid advance of the Germans in motor lorries had left them barely enough time to feed their horses before escaping. He continued his account:

> As we came near the Marne our troop, along with the 9th Lancers, advanced into a small village, and we did not know the danger we were in until shower of bullets and shells came over us. Then we realised that the Germans were only few hundred yards away. We were small in number, so we had to retreat over open country. The shell fire was terrible. I had a narrow escape from death, as a bullet penetrated my mess-tin, which I had strapped to my side. The Lancers lost a few of their men, but we were lucky, as we only lost a horse or two.

> Next the battle of the Aisne came off, and we were between two shell fires, for a fortnight. On one occasion our officer sent a corporal and myself out on patrol duty to a deserted village. The shells began to fly in all directions, and as I was standing at a tree a shell came and took the top of it away. There was no one in the village, and everything was in flames. I saw one poor fellow killed beyond where I was posted, we had to stick it until we got orders to leave. I would not like to be in a corner like it again.
>
> We had several attacks with those Uhlans, but we made short work of them. One day our officer sent four of us out on scouting duty. We were feeding our horses in a yard when a troop of German Lancers came into the town. I was on sentry at the gate, and gave the alarm, and we were soon out after them. They are great cowards. They flew from us like rabbits and cried for mercy, but we showed them very little, as they showed us none. I am not allowed to say where I am now, but we expect to be in Berlin at Christmas.[76]

By late September, Captain Maddick meanwhile was full of admiration for what his men had achieved. In his eyes it vindicated the British military system:

> I think that even these few weeks of war have conclusively proved that it is the training of the men that really counts, and that it is the long service that has enabled us, a tiny force, to hold the German hordes in check during the retreat from Mons. In the matter of shooting there is no comparison between the Germans and our men. The German marksmanship is vile; in fact, it is so bad that our men are absolutely contemptuous of it, and I'm afraid

this contempt may lead to a great loss of life for us, as the men seem to think a German can't possibly hit them at 200 yards.

To cast doubts on the bravery of the German privates is, in my opinion, wrong. They must be brave to come on in the attack, as they do in columns, to meet certain death. At first thought one wonders why they don't adopt our open formation, but second thoughts tell one the reason is that the German private cannot be trusted away from the immediate control of his officer. His discipline, unlike ours, is one of fear, and not affection, as with our men. He is a soldier by force, whether he likes it or not; while our men are soldiers from choice, and their profession is their pride.

To sum up, in my opinion, the great weak point of that really wonderful machine, the German army, is 'conscription', as it ruins the men. In a conscript army the majority of the men dread the time when they will be called upon to serve, and hate it the whole time they are serving, with the result that they only do what they are absolutely driven to do by the necessarily severe discipline. The longest period of service with the colours is three years, and how much can an unwilling man be trained in that time? The one thing he is thoroughly trained in is a hatred of his officers and N.C.O.s, with the result that in war he does not trust them, and they don't trust him.[77]

Again and again in the touch-and-go struggles that were to follow the Retreat from Mons, both on the Aisne and at Ypres, dismounted cavalrymen 'filled the gap', re-took captured trenches, or saved apparently impossible situations. By their unexpected arrival, fresh and dry-skinned in the muddy woods on the heights of the Aisne, they checked many of the enemy's concerted attempts to cut off the British infantry and artillery, and foiled every effort to recapture any of the bridges across the Aisne, only 2 or 3 miles behind them. Of entrenching tools they had none, so usually trenches they had none. One day Arthur Osburn and Colonel Mullens, not enjoying the splinters of the enemy's shells, were compelled to scrape a hole in the bank beneath some thorn bushes with jack-knives. On one of the critical days on the heights of the Aisne, west of Paissy, Osburn remembered passing along to the left a message that came to him from his right: 'Will "A" Squadron lend "C" Squadron the spade?' Many 'traditionalist' cavalry officers were uneasy about the way this campaign was developing; Archibald Home, writing in his diary for 27 September 1914, recorded:

> Alarmist message – Germans establishing themselves at the Oeuilly-Paissy crossroads – want us to turn them out. The General very funny about it, Cavalry charging a trench or crawling up with rifle in the hand and sword between the teeth like the pirate pictures one sees – this is Infantry work and not Cavalry.[78]

Towards the end of September, bayonets had been issued to cavalrymen for the first time. It was an acknowledgement that their role in this war was changing and that far from being a temporary aberration, fighting on foot was to become the norm for most of the time in this war. However, the Regular British cavalrymen were soon to be joined in action by some of their brethren from the Territorial Force Yeomanry regiments; in an echo of the Boer War the two branches of the army, professional and volunteer would come together on the battlefield, and the amateurs would prove to be as adept and hardy as any of their Regular comrades.

Chapter Four

The Race to the Sea

Following the stalemate on the Aisne the two sides battled to find an open flank, which resulted in the so called 'race to the sea'. The BEF was redeployed to the left of the French line and from 30 September the regiments of the Cavalry Corps began moving north once more, marching in the evenings in the main to avoid observation by the enemy. In many cases this led them along the same roads down which they had retreated only weeks before. Archibald Home however observed how different the demeanour of the men was, now that they were advancing. Previously they were despondent and dragged their feet, now heads were high and the men alert.

Meanwhile, the British 3rd Cavalry Division, which had been intended as reinforcements for the British and Belgian troops at Antwerp, had landed at Ostend; however the former city fell to the Germans before they could reach it. Marching east, these British troops were in the vicinity of Ghent when they encountered the Belgian field army moving west. The military situation was at this point very fluid, and they were also just as likely to meet Germans (particularly cavalry patrols) as there were no front lines as such. The advanced guard of the 3rd Cavalry Division was provided by several regiments, in particular the 1st (Royal) Dragoons. Private John Cusack was one of the regiment's scouts; he was from Glasgow and had joined the army aged 15, serving initially with the 2nd Dragoons (Scots Greys) before transferring to the Royals. During pre-war service he had trained as a regimental scout, and now having landed in Belgium on 8 October he and another trooper ranged ahead, on the lookout for and reporting

German movements. As they made their way across country heading ultimately now to Ypres, they encountered the straggling remains of the Belgian army, and also a ubiquitous character who seemed to be everywhere. Cusack remembered that:

> A remarkable man called Commander Samson, who was – or had been – with a naval reserve unit, dashed on to our scene. The Commander was a little rotund, weather-beaten man, in naval uniform with a 'Captain Kettle' beard and whiskers, driving round in a Rolls-Royce armoured lorry, the size of a taxi. He had mounted on it a three-pounder gun on a pivot, and he had a sailor with him as his driver. He told us, 'We've just come out from Antwerp. Makin' ourselves a bit useful with this naval armoured car!' Round his hat he had a white band, on which he had painted, in black, '2,000 MARKS'. He said, 'That's the price the Germans have put on my head if they capture me.'[79]

When it became evident that Antwerp would have to be abandoned, the armoured cars were given the task of harassing the Germans who were approaching the escape route to Ostend. After this, Samson continued to work with the British cavalry, providing reconnaissance information as to German movements, until the front line finally settled to the east of Ypres. Cusack continued:

> Whenever we made contact with a German patrol within his gun range, he would thank us and then, rapping out some nautical order like 'Action on the starboard quarter', he would fire several rounds at the Germans with his three-pounder. He never stayed to receive acknowledgement when the Germans fired back, and it was we who unfortunately bore the brunt of his reprisals.

> He had an assistant called Major Ed Haynes, who had got out of Antwerp with him, and was also scouting round in an armoured Rolls-Royce with a machine-gun. We liked to see them, because they were the only people who gave us any reliable information about the enemy's positions. One day Samson came bowling up in his armoured car with two Uhlan lances propped up on the front of it and trussed to the gun itself was an Uhlan prisoner. Samson was gaily wearing his prisoner's helmet.[80]

Winston Churchill, who had conceived the idea of landing troops at Ostend and Antwerp, thought these troops provided reinforcements at a vital moment. His strongly held view was that but for the support offered to the Belgian army, and for the measures taken to prolong their resistance, the considerable German forces engaged in that country would have been free to carry out an almost uninterrupted march upon the Channel ports.

While the infantry of the BEF moved north from the Aisne by bus and train, the cavalry led the way through long and trying marches. Every so often there was a ten minute halt for tea, one man making tea for his troop whilst his comrades tended his horse. Corporal Lawrence of the 12th Lancers remembered:

> The tea maker would get water from anywhere. It was dubious liquid at times (we never used water from our water-bottles if we could help it), and was boiled and skimmed, boiled and skimmed, before the tea was added. ... The tea was always consumed by the time 'saddle-up' or 'girth-up' was ordered. Quick work; always done in silence; no comment; everybody did something to help.[81]

The battle re-commenced in earnest on 11 October 1914. Some woods to the north of the Bethune – Aire canal held by German mounted troops were cleared by the British cavalry, and they then pushed the enemy back through Fletre and Le Coq de Paille. A major action took place at the Mont des Cats, which offered considerable advantages to the enemy in terms of observation. The Trappist monastery here was situated at the top of a 518 foot hill. The 3rd Cavalry Brigade under Brigadier General Vaughan was ordered to take it and clear the surrounding woods which were in German hands at the time. The monastery itself was strongly held by troops from the German *3rd Kavallerie-Division*, who had dug trenches around the outside and were also in defensive positions inside the monastery. Vaughan ordered the 4th Hussars to attack from the west, and the 16th Lancers to approach from the east. The attacks would be co-ordinated by the Royal Horse Artillery, which at the designated time would shell a windmill adjacent to the monastery. The 5th Lancers were in reserve. Before the main attack took place however, three officers were killed by sniper fire whilst reconnoitring. The deaths of two, Major John Kirwen Gatacre and Lieutenant Francis Levita of the 4th Hussars, were described by their commanding officer in a letter to the latter's mother:

> [They] had been sent on a dangerous reconnaissance; and they rode together straight up to a big monastery on top of a hill, having had direct orders from the General to ascertain whether it was, or was not, held by the German troops. The Germans let them get up quite close and then suddenly opened up a hot fire at short range. The officers and the whole troop with them (about ten men) turned to gallop back under cover, when Gatacre was shot. Your boy pulled up at once and rode back to see if he could help him, but had only got a few yards when he, too, was shot. It was a gallant intention. And had he survived, I should have recommended him for a decoration. A few hours later the monastery was captured and the bodies of both Captain Gatacre and your boy were found where

they had been shot. Both must have fallen dead. The Germans had stripped them of everything except their actual clothes. I posted you the other day your boy's sword, which we happened to recover. We buried him with Gatacre in the monastery and the Rev. McGuinness, our brigade chaplain, has a record of the exact spot.[82]

Major John Kirwan Gatacre, King Edward's Own Lancers (Indian Army) attached 4th Hussars. He was killed on 13 October 1914 during a reconnaissance near Mont des Cats, Meteren. (Author's Collection)

Brigadier General Vaughan was infuriated by this incident, for which he blamed Major General Hubert Gough. The latter had met the reconnaissance party on the way up, and told them that he did not believe any enemy were present inside the monastery. Whether this caused the officers to be unduly reckless may never be known.

Upon the signal to attack, the 16th Lancers took off at the gallop, dismounted and opened fire on the German defenders. After about a quarter of an hour these men had had enough and began to fall back. Covered by their machine guns the 16th Lancers charged the enemy trenches, and shortly afterwards the monastery was in British hands. The Trappist monks had been present throughout the fighting, and it was recounted that the excitement of the incident caused them to break their vow of silence, and now they would not stop talking!

On 13 October the 4th Hussars and 5th Lancers advanced on Hill 68 but were held up by enemy fire from scattered farms around the base. Upon the arrival of infantry reinforcements, these Germans withdrew at the end of the day. On 14 October the high ground above Berthen was secured. By now General Allenby was in command and ordered the whole of the Cavalry Corps to advance eastwards and reconnoitre the line of the River Lys. During the following two days the reconnaissance was carried out in the face of stiff opposition especially along the lower line of the river. On 16 October a general advance eastwards was ordered along the whole of the British Armentières-La Bassée front, in an effort to keep up the pressure on the Germans. The Cavalry Corps in the north was ordered to attempt to force its way across the River Lys, with the 2nd Cavalry Brigade in the vanguard, but it was largely unsuccessful, finding most of the crossings either blown up or heavily defended. Home recorded:

> This sounds like another battle of the Aisne. It is very hard work on the Cavalry man, he goes into the fight with no reserves and occupies a front which four times the number of infantry would require. He is quite cheerful about it, he only grumbles when he has to come out of it.[83]

2723 Shoeing-Smith Walter Cockett 16th Lancers, who saw action in France after disembarking on 17 August 1914. (Author's Collection)

So far there had been little opposition, the enemy having been apparently frightened out of his commanding positions to the west of the Lys, but he was expected to react strongly as soon as his reinforcements arrived. It was decided, therefore, to try to force the passage of the river before they came. An excellent patrol by Lieutenant Wernher of the 12th Lancers brought back valuable information of the state of the defences and bridges over the canal and the Lys, but the attempt on them failed. Those in the regiment who had lately been complaining of too little now found plenty to do, digging trenches without tools and forming a sniping line to hold the ground already occupied. They were to find, also, that this was quite a different kind of warfare from that of the months before, the high-wired fences, the numerous by-roads and many farms being far more dangerous and deadly than the open downs of the past. The Germans quickly adapted themselves to this country. Another officer of the 12th Lancers, Lieutenant Leslie wrote on 17 October:

> The way they let the men go past and wait for the officers is disconcerting ... entering villages which are occupied is hell, as they shoot the officers from houses, and numerous officers have been killed in this way.[84]

Heavy enemy resistance was met with, and the British cavalry had to be largely content with holding the railway track to the west of the river, as the infantry came up and began to take over more of the line. Lieutenant T.L. Horn was the machine gun officer of the 16th Lancers and has left a dramatic account of the attempt to take Warneton, north of Armentières, as part of this drive. The town was still very much intact and there was severe house-to-house street fighting, with the Germans also firing from behind barricades. He wrote:

> [at 4.30 pm] it was … decided that we should attack the centre of the village, which was barricaded. One of my

[machine] guns had been placed on a roof overlooking the barricade, a hole being knocked through the tiles. The plan was that one [field] gun of 'E' Battery [Royal Horse Artillery] was to be manhandled up a side street, and then pushed quickly round the corner and fired at the barricade, under cover of my M.G. firing from the roof, and then one troop of 'C' Squadron was to rush the barricade, backed up if necessary by the rest of 'C' Squadron and half of 'A' Squadron. It was quite dark by the time all this was arranged.

We were all standing along the sides of the street, with a certain amount of odd sniping going on towards the village centre, when the gun went off – I've never heard such a row – a deafening crash, and then the breaking and falling of glass all over and around one, as of course every window was broken to pieces, and most of the houses were three stories high. Three shells were fired, and then 'C' squadron rushed and took the barricade … a good deal of shooting was going on from windows and doorways: it was pitch dark and one couldn't tell where it was coming from or who was shooting, as one could see the flash from a rifle whether it was being fired towards one or from one, also wherever the bullet struck a brick or stone there was a flash. On reaching the centre square there was another barricade down a right handed street leading to the canal: one M.G. was placed at the corner so that it could fire at this, and the man could lean round and have a look occasionally, but could fire it from behind the corner, merely putting his hand out to press the button. I took the other gun across to the opposite side of the square, each of us being covered in turn as we ran across, by the gun already in position ...

All this time there was odd shooting going on, and all the side roads were being barricaded and picketed.

> A big house was on fire on our side of the square, making any movement visible, but luckily one had also caught fire near their barricade, and they couldn't move much without being seen. Suddenly a 'Verey' flare light came over and dropped almost into the square, lighting up everything as though it was daylight: it was our first experience of them, and one could see everyone crouching as close to the walls as possible, wondering what was going to happen next, personally I thought when it touched the ground there would be an awful explosion, but of course nothing of the sort happened … The next item was a machine-gun opening fire from their barricade onto my other gun, which promptly replied, and it was the most extraordinary though horrid sight to see these two M.G.s like a couple of angry cats spitting at each other not more than 25 yards apart, sparks flying wherever the bullets hit the cobbles or walls, and the noise of course being deafening. Thank goodness our gun had been set up and laid when not under fire, whereas their gun had been brought up under fire and consequently badly aimed ...[85]

These operations were continued throughout 17, 18 and 19 October. Strong enemy forces prevented the Cavalry Corps from securing a permanent footing on the eastern bank of the river. At the northern end of this front the Cavalry Corps was ordered to secure the important high ground to the east of the Mont des Cats. Instead they met determined German resistance from the direction of Meteren; the village was well sited for defence, its church tower offering good observation to the enemy, and the cavalry, unable to turn the Germans out, asked for infantry assistance. Among those killed on 17 October was Lieutenant John Eden of the 12th Lancers, the eldest brother of future Prime Minister Sir Anthony Eden. The death of Lieutenant

Officers of the 16th Lancers, seen in Dublin before the outbreak of war. Middle row, fourth from left is Lieutenant T.L. Horne. (Author's Collection)

Eden is well chronicled in the regimental history and the diary of Captain H.V.S. Charrington:

> On the morning of 17th October 1914, C Squadron saddled up at 5.30am and took up an outpost line from GAPAARD to GARDE DIEU and was instructed to put its patrols well forward to watch the river Lys between COMINES and WARNETON. B Squadron were sent forward to TEN-BRIELEN, also with its patrols well forward.
>
> The Belgian countryside was full of German cyclist and infantry patrols, who laid up behind hedges and buildings. The countryside was very enclosed compared to the open fields of France. The terrain was ideal for defence and provided great advantage over mounted men who had to stick to the roads as each of the fields was bounded either by deep and un-jumpable ditches and wire fences.

Lt. Eden's troop was sent to clear up a very difficult situation near America [1.5km NE of Comines] and was ambushed as they entered the village. The Germans allowed the first 2 riders to enter the village and engaged the patrol at very close range with a Maxim Machine Gun. Lt. Eden and one of his soldiers Pte. Fred Hart were killed instantly. The rest of the patrol escaped by jumping fences. Pte. Wilmot was captured but the Germans, after taking everything from him, chased him away. The remainder of the patrol were collected together and returned home under somewhat difficult circumstances with Cpl. Branch. For this action and an act of personal gallantry at Wytschaet the following month, he was awarded the DCM. After much rumour as to the fate of Lt. Eden, a patrol of the 20th Hussars eventually found John's body, the Germans having already removed his boots, cap and coat. The Hussars buried him where he lay.[86]

British cavalry moving forward into action, 1914. (Author's Collection)

The officers of C Squadron of the 1st (Royal) Dragoons kept a diary which chronicled the actions of their unit, and which picks up on events after Cusack's account. In it they recorded the open nature of the fighting to the east of Ypres as the front had yet to settle into static warfare:

> Oct 19th: Concentrated at Moorslede at 6am then proceeded to make a reconnaissance to the East. Opposition was met with immediately on crossing the Roulers-Menin road, where A&B Squadrons had some sharp fighting. Several casualties occurring. The Household Cavalry on our left met with a very superior force of German infantry, and the 7th Division on our right were also hung up. The troops on both flanks were finally forced to retire, and we soon discerned German infantry attacking our left, so we had to give ground.
>
> One troop of C Squadron, Lieutenant de Trafford's, had to remain until the last, and narrowly escaped being cut off. The German infantry had advanced in force to within some 200 yards before he got on his horses. Luckily an armoured car in charge of Second Lieutenant P. Poole R.W.F. with Maxim, stopped while the horses were being mounted, and thereby saved the situation.
>
> On retiring Lieutenant de Trafford's horse was shot under him, and he was thrown on his head and sustained concussion. An ambulance picked him up and brought him in. The rest of the troop having one other horse hit got away unscathed. That night the whole brigade billeted at Poelcapelle, arriving there very late.
>
> Oct 20th: Left Poelcapelle at 4am & proceeded to Westrozebeke to dig a line of entrenchments and hold a line until the arrival of the 1st Army who were expected in the afternoon. French troops were on our left and

> the Household Cavalry on our right. The position was heavily shelled all the morning. The French gave way on our left, so we had to draw back to meet the 1st Army coming up. The Germans followed us up rigorously and finally entered Poelcapelle. The advanced troops of the 1st Army only reached St Julien that night. C Squadron had to hold a crossroads north of St Julien all that night. Langemarck was attacked early in the evening and there was heavy fighting at Zonnebeke most of the night. Patrols of the enemy came very close to our lines and we opened fire several times. It was a very dark night and very difficult to distinguish anything. A company of the Coldstream Guards came up to support us if attacked. At 3pm we sent the horses back quietly a couple of miles.[87]

The following day C Squadron re-joined the rest of the Royal Dragoons at Ypres, before going into the trenches at Zandvoorde to relieve the Scots Guards.

As the 3rd Cavalry Division from Ostend and those regiments that had come up from the south stood together, there were many opportunities to renew old friendships from before the war, and share news of more recent events. With the Belgian army now holding the North Sea coast and the line of the Yser Canal, the French holding the ground to the north of Ypres, and the British holding the sector from Ypres south to Armentières, the front line now ran continuously from the Franco-Belgian border to the sea. All hope of the German armies outflanking the allies had now gone. Their only chance of seizing a quick victory in the west now lay in smashing their way through and seizing the Channel ports, which would cut the British Army off from its supplies. The stage was set for the first major clash on the Western Front, as the Germans made an all out effort to break through at Ypres.

Chapter Five

The Stand at Ypres

The Ypres battlefield of 1914 was almost totally obliterated (both physically and in the British national consciousness) by the later battles which took place over the same ground. The waterlogged, shell scarred and crated wilderness of 1917 has entered the national memory as the image of the First World War, but in 1914 things were very different. The countryside to the south-east of Ypres, where the cavalrymen would make their stand was dotted with woods, forming an almost continuous chain from Zonnebeke to Wytschaete. As well as mature trees, they contained dense undergrowth and provided a good deal of cover for the movement of troops, and for attacking formations to assemble. In addition, most of the villages which ringed Ypres were substantially intact at this time, again providing cover to infantry. Between these villages were farmsteads, and open fields containing sugar beet or sometimes cereals. In these fields, cover was provided by drainage ditches or haystacks. This then was the terrain over which the coming battle would be fought.

The early clashes around Ypres began on 19 Octobcr, when British troops, still hoping to push forward, had run into the cavalry screen of superior German forces moving west. On 20 October the Germans launched a general attack along the whole of the British front. The 3rd Cavalry Division at this point occupied positions to the north-east of Ypres, near Passchendaele, but also on 20 October in order to protect the open British flank, 1st Cavalry Brigade had been ordered to occupy the village of Messines, approximately 5 miles south of Ypres. They got there just in time, to find the village unoccupied by the enemy. Even at this early point in the fighting, the tactical importance of this village had been noted by Archibald Home, but he was confident that Brigadier General Briggs and his men would hold on here, and so it proved.

The Germans continued their policy of attacking everywhere simultaneously, and 21 October was a day of ferocious assaults along the whole British line. Heavy blows fell against the 4th Dragoon Guards on the edge of Ploegsteert Wood. Some Germans had penetrated the wood and the situation appeared critical until the arrival of parties of the 9th Lancers as reinforcements. Captain Francis Grenfell of this regiment wrote:

Lieutenant-Colonel E.B. Cook MVO, 1st Life Guards, mortally wounded by a shell at Zandvoorde on 22 October 1914. (Author's Collection)

> Our present job is pretty disheartening. We go forward and capture positions for the infantry, who are entrenched four miles behind and move terribly slow. We are then withdrawn, and have again to recapture the same position next day. Eventually the infantry come up and take the place, assisted by divisional artillery the same place we took three days before with a squadron ... We have started the same old game as at the Aisne, and we have had five of the hardest days of the war in trenches repelling German attacks. It has become such a recognized idea to use us for this work as soon as we get in touch with the enemy that I am afraid all the cavalry traditions are for ever ended, and we have become mounted infantry pure and simple, with very little of the mounted about it.[88]

Further south the British 2nd Cavalry Division was also heavily attacked from 9.30 am, being shelled out if its trenches. As the battle intensified the 3rd Cavalry Division was relieved from its position in the north by French troops and took up the line between Zandvoorde and the Ypres-Comines railway. To its south lay the 2nd Cavalry Division covering the gap between Hollebeke and Messines, and holding Messines itself were the 1st Cavalry Division. For the previous four or five days on a British front of some 20 miles the only reserve was perhaps 2,000 men, and the Cavalry Corps had been fighting on a front of 6 miles with no reserve at all, all its men were in the firing line. It was a dangerous game of bluff, for if the Germans had chosen to focus on any particular point, instead of attacking all along the front simultaneously, then there would have been little to hold them.

The consequence of this of course was that the men of the Cavalry Corps were now urgently in need of rest. They had been in action day and night for five days, and this could not continue. However the imminent arrival of the Indian Corps offered hope of some relief. Although the standard of training and musketry of individual cavalrymen was high, the corps was hampered to some extent by the fact that its men were supported by the lighter 13-pounder guns of the Royal Horse Artillery, and lacked the fire power available to the infantry through their supporting 18-pounder batteries. This was remedied to some extent on 27 October when a heavy artillery battery and some 6-inch howitzers were made available.

On 29 October the Germans renewed their attacks around Ypres, and these also grew in intensity. Once again Messines was the keystone of the British defence in the southern portion of the line and the 1st Cavalry Division were in the thick of the fighting. Home tells us:

> The Cavalry have had to do most things but street fighting with bayonets is quite new. We had a Brigade of Cavalry and some Native Infantry [i.e. Indian troops] for the

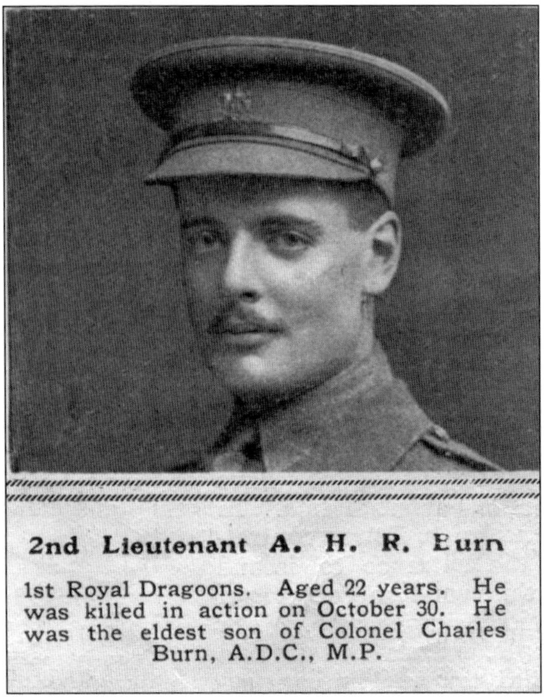

Second Lieutenant A.H.R. Burn, 1st (Royal) Dragoons, Killed in action 29 October 1914 (Author's Collection)

> defence. We held our original line round the south and east of the town. The Germans then made up their minds that they would take Messines and commenced the attack quite systematically in their usual way.[89]

The defence of Messines was one of the most remarkable episodes in the First Battle of Ypres. Against enormous odds the cavalry held it largely with the bayonet, fighting from house to house and street corner to street corner for two days, the whole time under constant shell fire, the artillery rounds dropping at a rate of about fifty per minute at the peak of the struggle. Trooper Frederick Sinnock of the 2nd Life Guards was from Littlehampton, Sussex, and had arrived in France just in time to take part in the retreat from Mons. Surviving for five or six days on what they could find to eat in the surrounding fields, his horse carried him nearly 60 miles on one particular day. When the advance resumed, he was soon in action at Ypres, and recalled that:

> The work was more that of Mounted Infantry than cavalry. At Messines we not only had to handle the rifle and the bayonet instead of the sabre, but we also had to use the spade and dig our own trenches; with all our men six feet in height we had to dig a good way down to make trenches of any real value![90]

After surviving the action at Messines, ironically Sinnock was invalided home when he was kicked severely by a horse. Further east along the British line was Trooper Albert Courtney, whose home address was 30 Iris Street, Belfast. Courtney had formerly served with the Inniskilling Dragoons and became a reservist on his return from India earlier in 1914. He was employed as a nurse in the Royal Victoria Hospital and it was whilst working in this role that he was called up upon the outbreak of hostilities, and posted to the 1st Life Guards. In the course of the operations around Ypres he was severely wounded on 29 October. In an interview with the *Belfast Telegraph* he had no hesitation in saying that he owed his life to the gallantry of two other British soldiers:

> We got an order to retire in single file and when I got to the vicinity of a farm house one shell burst behind me and another in front, with the result that I was struck with shrapnel both in the left leg and in the back. I lay prostrate and could hardly breathe. Indeed I thought I was done for completely. If it had not been for the pluck of two comrades, George Ford and another, I am quite certain that I should never have seen home again. When Ford and the other brave fellow came to my assistance, knowing the grave danger they were running, I told them to go on, but not withstanding the terrible risk they were running, for the Maxim bullets were coming fast, they picked me up and carried me – under fire all the time – to a doctor a good half-mile away. The medico, who was attending to patients behind a haystack, dressed my wounds, and afterwards, with the assistance of a number of others, carried me two miles to a horse ambulance, in which I was taken a further three miles, to a motor ambulance. In the latter I was brought into the town of Ypres and after further treatment there was taken three hours later to Boulogne. For ten days I remained in the Australian voluntary hospital there, being afterwards sent to Colchester, whence I came home on sick furlough.[91]

Unlike many others, he expressed the opinion that the war would last a considerable time, adding that he fully expected that when recovered he would have to go back to the front. Trooper Will Gostelow, also of the 1st Life Guards, from Bradwell, Buckinghamshire had numerous lucky escapes in this action, which he described:

Since writing to you last we have changed our position considerably. We were in the train two days, and then we met the Germans in large numbers in the town of ----- in Belgium, which they held. The Household Cavalry was put in a line right across the place, and there we lay for 48 hours in a turnip field in the cold and rain. At last the Germans came on in swarms. We were not enough for them, and we had to retreat. As soon as we got up to run they were on top of us, and the bullets simply poured round us, several of them going through my cloak. But not one of them hit my body. It was hellish. You can imagine something of what it was like in this turnip field with the shells dropping near enough to bury me in the mud and dirt they threw up. I laid in one of the holes which a shell made near me. This offered more cover for me. Then we had a run of nearly two miles to our horses, dead beat. During this run we were being 'fed' with shrapnel, and I could run no further. I was completely exhausted so I walked as well as I could.

The fellows were falling all round me and a piece of shell whizzed past my head. It struck another chap in the leg, and I have since heard that he died from loss of blood. Not satisfied with this, the enemy dropped several shells among the horses, killing some and wounding others. That night I slept under a haystack. When the horses arrived the next morning we went and took up another position, and this time we dug ourselves in deep trenches. We still hold that position, and in fact we now defy a million Germans. In 48 hours they (the enemy) made about six attacks on our position, but we held them back each time. We have lost about five officers and about thirty men dead and wounded. Another fellow and I [were] told to take some ammunition to the trenches as our fellows were getting short. We got the boxes to

> the trenches on our hands and knees, and whilst we were in a ditch the bullets simply buzzed round us like flies. I shall never forget these last four days. I am perfectly happy and there is nothing for you worry about. I bear a charmed life, or I would have been shot before now.[92]

Further to the south, with his regiment, the 4th Dragoon Guards, was Lieutenant Norman Thwaites, who wrote:

> On October 30th, we found ourselves in Messines, that picturesque little town in which some weeks before we had billeted in great comfort. This second visit was a very different affair. The old abbey was already battered to pieces; only those walls erected nearly a millennium ago had withstood the German guns. Street after street we lost until forced to the very extremity of the town. Here we formed barricades,

L1097 Trooper Frederick Lowe Ryder, 17th Lancers, who was hospitalised on 30 October 1914. A recalled reservist, he was probably seconded to the Life Guards as his regiment was still en route from India at the time. (Author's Collection)

awaiting desperately the promised French support. In the market square, where we held the enemy for a time, a group of men sheltering behind a wall were torn to pieces by a huge shell which came though the masonry.[93]

7030 Trooper Charles Bunyon, 5th Lancers, seen in a German PoW camp following his capture on 30 October 1914. He has lost his original cap badge and replaced it with a 5 from a German uniform. (Author's Collection)

The second day of the battle for Messines came on 30 October. Massed German attacks were about to be made, in order to place the British and their French allies under simultaneous pressure along most of the length of the line around Ypres. The day was thus notable as the Germans now attacked on a wider front, and the battle was to spread southwards, once again to include the positions held by the Cavalry Corps. The troops likely to bear the brunt of the assault had spent the previous night reinforcing their positions as best they could, but the reality of the situation was that much of the British front line consisted of no more than a series of isolated posts, worryingly vulnerable to a surging German attack which had the potential to force its way between them, were not the enemy kept at rifle range. The weakest portion of the line was that held by the three divisions of the Cavalry Corps, whose squadrons by now numbered on average only eighty rifles each, on the southern flank of the Salient at Zandevoorde. The dismounted cavalrymen had taken up positions in ditches, inside abandoned houses and behind haystacks as they awaited the onslaught. As one British officer put it, all they could hope to do was 'putty up the holes' by throwing in reinforcements wherever the Germans broke through.

The attack began very differently from that of the previous day. For over an

Shoeing-Smith Herbert Sowden, 1st (Royal) Dragoons, killed in action on 30 October 1914. (Author's Collection)

hour from 6.45 am the fire of over 200 German heavy guns rained down around Zandvoorde in the north of the Cavalry Corps sector. This in itself caused much destruction but at 8.00 am it was followed by an overwhelming infantry assault. The cavalrymen were forced back on to their reserve positions. Among those units heavily attacked here was the 2nd Life Guards. The Second World War intelligence chief and wartime head of MI6, Major General Stewart Menzies, served as a Lieutenant and adjutant of the regiment. In a letter written after the war he outlined his recollections of that day:

> On the 30th the Household Cavalry Regiments were in the front line... When the German attack was launched the 7th Division on the left were driven back, and the 2nd Life Guards on the right were also compelled to retire, I believe to conform with the retirement of troops on their right. Beyond the above practically nothing is known of what occurred as the two squadrons and the machine-guns of the 'Blues' completely disappeared, and only very few survivors were taken prisoner, and on their return at the end of the war they were unable, I understand, to throw much light on the attack.
>
> My Regiment had an officer who was on the extreme left who managed to escape with slight wounds. According to his story which was somewhat confused owing to his being dazed, the attack was made by German infantry after a very heavy preliminary bombardment. I can only conclude that the squadrons were cut off owing to their somewhat forward position, and were ultimately all killed, though it is remarkable that there should have been so few wounded taken prisoner. Some of the trenches were very primitive, and I remember that one was much too deep to allow of the occupants seeing over the top, and they would hardly be in a position to

> offer any effective resistance. But on the other hand other trenches were quite well sighted, and the whole incident has always struck me as one of the most remarkable occurrences of the war. I fear that one must assume that the Germans behaved in an ultra-Hunlike manner and gave no quarter. According to one N.C.O. they did not trouble to remove the wounded who were left out, and he attributed his being taken to the German dressing-station to the fact that he was wearing a pair of leather gloves and may therefore have been mistaken for an officer.[94]

Slightly to the north, German attacks near Hollebeke on 30 October had come to nothing – their heavy guns had inflicted little damage on the scattered cavalrymen and German infantry had made only half-hearted progress. Towards noon however the attack on Hollebeke village intensified. Some of the cavalry fell back (in good order it must be said) but the centre of the resistance in this part of the line rested on the defence of the bridge over the Ypres-Comines canal, which had not been destroyed by the Royal Engineers due to a shortage of explosives. The canal represented a significant obstacle and the Germans threw in attack after attack in an attempt to reach the bridge but all were thrown back. That the bridge was held so resolutely was in no small part due to the bravery of Lieutenant K.C. North of the 4th Hussars, who with one squadron and the Maxim detachment defended it all day. North was killed in the process by a shell, but part of the citation for his DSO read:

> The enemy were unable to reach the bridge, largely owing to Lieutenant North's handling of his machine guns. One of these was knocked to bits and Lieutenant North was killed [but] the bridge remained in our possession until the 4th Hussars were relieved.[95]

Lieutenant Kenneth North, 4th Hussars, who held the bridge over the Ypres-Comines Canal at Hollebeke with two machine guns on 30 October 1914. (Author's Collection)

A remarkable and rare German photograph of the bridge held by Lieutenant North. (Author's Collection)

Meanwhile the 11th Hussars were hanging on under terrific fire, and Trooper Edward Russell, of this regiment, told of his own dramatic experiences. While in action in the trenches at Messines the calf of one his legs was blown clean away by a shrapnel shell, and in the trench beside where be lay another, 'Jack Johnson' shell buried alive an officer, sergeant, and fifty men. He remembered:

> They were digging for them afterwards, and could only take them out in pieces, they were all killed.[96]

Russell was picked up his comrades, and handed over to a couple of RAMC men. As he was being taken along a road at night time the enemy's shells and machine gun fire raked it, and the men bringing the stretcher dropped it and Russell in the road, and ran away for shelter:

> I couldn't walk, of course, and just rolled over to the side of the road, then dragged myself along for hours until I came to our barricades, where I was put on another stretcher and token to hospital.[97]

A more detailed description of the ongoing fighting in the south of the cavalry sector comes from Trooper Ethelbert Minton, also of the 11th Hussars, who wrote to a local newspaper at home:

> Our squadron, along with the rest of the _____ were occupying the town of Messines, in Belgium, a strategic point in our line, and had been there for many days. Our horses were some miles in the rear and we were stretched along a line of trenches just outside the town. The town was further defended by barricades etc. in the streets. The ____ relieved us every two days to enable us to get a sleep. The town and vicinity were bombarded all day by

4801 Trooper Henry Edward Wood, 3rd Hussars, killed in action on 30 October 1914. (Author's Collection)

the heavy howitzers of the Germans, immense damage was done and the town fired in several places. Little damage to us until 2 pm on Friday last [30 October], when shells started falling all along in front of the trench occupied by our squadron, making the ground rock like an earthquake. At last one fell not five yards from me, but did not hit me, owing to a buttress of the trench being in the way.

I crept round into the crater made by the shell and found the officer and men next to me buried alive. Saw a tuft of the man's hair sticking out, and cleared the dirt away from his mouth so that he could get his breath. Dug him out and half dug the officer out, but found he was dead. The man had his leg smashed frightfully. I made a

> tourniquet of handkerchiefs and bound his leg to a long stick. He has been saved, and my bandages were left on by the doctor, who simply added another splint. Shells fell along the trench, burying the whole of the ____troop alive. I went to them with a message, and saw it myself. The squadron still hung on, and we prayed for night to come. Every moment we expected to be rushed by German infantry. The sergeant-major was killed. Sergeant F. took over his work and posted me as 'look out'. I was sick with the horror of it, for the first time in the war. Just on nightfall we were again bombarded and lost more men. Finally we had to evacuate the trench. During this the captain told Sergeant F. to send two reliable men, volunteers, to see if the Germans were attempting to come up to the trenches we had left. Sergeant F. said 'I'll go, sir, and I can answer for Minton coming with me'. So I went back again, but no sign of the Germans. We then reoccupied the trenches, the bombardment having passed us. I call them trenches, but by this time they were just tumbled heaps and holes.[98]

At nightfall after forty-eight hours in the trenches, in 6 inches of water, without food, in pouring rain, and under constant shell fire, they were all relieved by the 9th Lancers, also dismounted. Minton continues:

> Instead of much-needed rest we had to man the barricade in the town all night. Next morning (Saturday), a general bombardment began again. The trenches we were in the night before, now occupied by the ____were first shelled by the Germans, as we had been, and finally carried by an enormous force of infantry. The same trenches were re-taken by a savage counter-attack by Indian troops. They charged with the bayonet and re-took the position, which

Major E.H.A. Abadie of the 9th (Queen's) Royal Lancers who was killed in action on 30 October 1914 at Messines, near Ypres. (Author's Collection)

had lost all resemblance to a trench. They in turn were driven out with awful losses, under a shower of frightful shells. My squadron was retired into the great courtyard of the monastery. The immense howitzer shells fell here again. A wall collapsed, burying two more men. Our number was now reduced to about 40. We dashed across the courtyard, one at a time, into the street beyond. Here we crouched under the wall, awaiting orders.

Suddenly, six immense shells fell right in the street at equal intervals and at the same moment. The concussion was awful. The air was filled with red brick-dust, so that you could not see your arms length in front of you. Walls came crashing down, and I heard most dreadful shouts.

> running wild, and burning villages, are common sights, and we are getting used to them.
>
> The guns have been roaring away now for a fortnight without rest. We ourselves, however, are fit and happy. I never felt better in my life. Although you'd think I had gloves on by the dirt on my hands. They are simply filthy, and my face is not much better. The food I am glad to say is very plentiful and good. No one can complain about it; at least I can't. some of the chaps do, but they are not good foragers and don't look after themselves. I had stewed chicken and vegetables the other night. Chickens are only a franc (10d) each, and we often buy them. The vegetables abound all over the countryside. The only things I miss are cigarettes (Gold Flake) and chocolate.[102]

The most critical day of the battle for Ypres, possibly also the most critical day of the 1914 campaign, and certainly one of the most critical days of the entire war for the British came on 31 October. It dawned unusually warm and clear, and for the first time in Flanders the Germans were able to use the balloon referred to above to direct the fire of the heavy artillery, with devastating effect. The main effort of the Germans on this day was directed towards the high ground of the Messines-Wytschaete ridge, in the southern half of the Salient. The village of Messines, at the southern end of the sector, still stood like a bastion in the British line. The village was defended by the remnants of three cavalry regiments, and a barricade constructed across the centre of the village was witness to bitter fighting as attack after attack was hurled at it. Captain Charles Blackburne of the 5th Dragoon Guards, described his part in the fighting for the town on this day in a letter to his brother:

> I had only just been back to report that we were driving [the Germans] back when I got word that we were to fall

back, as on our left they had pressed our line in. There had been a very strong attack there. It was very disappointing, as we were doing well on our side. We fell back, holding the town street by street. In the evening we re-occupied our side of the town and an attempt was made by some fresh troops to get round the flanks. But we had nothing like sufficient troops to do this as the Germans had pushed forward their whole line at this point. We held on to the side of the town we had fallen back to and there we were, Germans in one part and we in the other. We put up barricades across the street and they pushed a gun up to within a couple of hundred yards down the street and fired away at the barricade and adjoining houses, fairly bringing the place down about our ears.

My squadron was there until midnight, when we were relieved by other troops who held on until next day, but obviously it was only a question of time before we should have to evacuate it. If only we had been strong enough on the left to have held on we should have repulsed them. But once the left had to fall back we on the right were done, as they would have cut us off. Of course this is quite a small affair from the point of view of the whole show, and the falling back a kilometre at one point is of no consequence, but naturally we hated having to go when at our actual front we had driven them back.

Our regiment did well and there were many brave things done that day. We had a good many casualties. Poor Captain Whitchurch was killed. He was a very good and brave officer, Wiley wounded; Collier Johnson bruised by a wall falling upon him, but he will be back, I hope, in a few days. At the moment, however, I have not a single officer in the squadron, so it is a bit of an anxious time. There is no doubt, however, that the Germans had far the

> worst of it. My squadron alone must have accounted for one or two hundred. I thought I would tell you about it, as you know just how I am feeling. I am very fit, and much looking forward to getting a wee bit of rest.[103]

The pressure also continued on the northern part of the line, in the 7th Cavalry Brigade sector. Trooper William Stinchcombe of the Royal Horse Guards (Blues) wrote home to his local newspaper in the following terms:

> In the recent fight at Messines we held the trenches alongside the Indian troops and we kept relieving each other. The Indians are a smart lot of fellows. They are simply marvellous in creeping along the ground in an attack. On Saturday [31 October], during the early hours of the morning, the Germans attacked our trenches but we held them back, and must have caused heavy losses to the enemy, until we had run short of ammunition. By that time they had surrounded our trenches, so we had to retreat... Whilst retiring, I was wounded in the left cheek with a shrapnel bullet, which went right through the cheek.[104]

Another Royal Horse Guards soldier, Trooper C. Griffiths of D Squadron, from Conisbrough near Doncaster, wrote to his wife of the fighting in which he was involved:

> The reason you do not see many Horse Guards in the casualty lists is that the Royal Horse Guards, First Life Guards, and Second Life Guards are chiefly composed of the biggest men of Dragoon and Hussar regiments transferred to them to make the Household Cavalry the proper strength, and when these men get killed, because they have not taken the trouble to write 'Horse Guards'

> on their identity discs, they go in the casualty lists as Dragoons and Hussars. We have lost a lot of both killed and injured … It is not war, it is simply slaughter, and I think when it is all over they ought to hang the Kaiser.
>
> It would make you shudder to see French, German, and British dead lying about the fields, and they can't be removed for shell fire, for the Germans do not respect the white flag. A party of six of us were ordered to fetch in the body of a certain Household Cavalry officer which had been lying in the field for about a week. We had to give it up; it would have been certain death for us to try and recover his body.
>
> We are not doing much cavalry work yet; it is all trench work. We are more like infantry, and fight with bayonets as well as swords. Three nights ago I thought we were going to use them. The German fire was awful; both rifles and guns. Twice they tried to break through us, but we repulsed them. Their shelling of our trenches was so accurate that some of us had to run for it. The Germans have made a mess of the towns and villages with their big guns; hardly a house is left, and the beautiful cathedral of Ypres, when we are fighting, they have played havoc with. But I think their game is almost over. A great many of us think it will be over by Christmas.[105]

In a further letter to his wife, Trooper Griffiths speaks of the hardships which had been encountered on account of the worsening autumn weather:

> We have had nothing but rain this last fortnight, and are up to our knees in mud. But we have just had a change in the weather, and now it is frost and snow. We are in the thickest and hardest battle that has been fought yet,

The grave of Major Henry William, Viscount Crichton, Royal Horse Guards, in Zandvoorde Cemetery. He was killed in action on 31 October 1914. (Courtesy of Patrick Gariepy)

> and the longest. I don't think it will be many more days before the Germans are on the retreat. It has been the very devil in the trenches this last fortnight. ... But for all the shelling they give us, our casualties are very slight—lost a few killed and wounded. One would think it impossible to live under such fire, for they keep it up until dark, and then divide their attention between the surrounding villages and camps. It is the same with our guns; our artillery shells them all night long.[106]

After the 4th Dragoon Guards had relieved the Oxfordshire Hussars at Messines, Lieutenant Norman Thwaites was again in the front line. By this time the British had been all but driven out, hanging on to one edge only. He wrote of the difficulties that he and his men had in fending off wave after wave of enemy attacks, as the cloying mud found its way into the breeches of their weapons, preventing them from firing:

> 'My rifle's jammed with dirt sir,' is the excuse. 'And so is mine sir'. Another and another man sings out that his rifle is clogged. But the enemy is creeping back to his cover. Our fellows redouble their energies.
>
> 'Fire at the hedge, 500 yard range!'
>
> Again I glance behind me. No sign of reinforcement.
>
> Suddenly a man beside me grunts and claps his hand to his face. He drops. Further along the trench a youngster is quietly wrapping a bandage around his forearm. He is cheerily blasphemous.
>
> 'I'm hit sir', says a man on my, left, suddenly sitting down. He is very white and coughs incessantly. A chest wound. Still further to the left another group of grey forms emerges determinedly. They come at the double, their bayonets fixed – 'Half left – 200 yards – rapid fire'.

> Again our rifles blaze. They check, and running right and left, bolt for cover!
>
> Instantly shelling begins again. The attack is repulsed! Wonderful fire control on the part of their artillery.
>
> At this moment I turned to Sergeant Sessions beside me. 'Well done lads, we've beaten them off!'
>
> I am conscious of a slight tap on the jaw, like the glancing blow of a boxing glove on the chin – no more. Then a slight pain under the ear and a gush of something warm down my neck.
>
> 'Good Lord, I'm hit!'
>
> The man next to me is splashed with blood. He looks at it with staring eyes. 'I'm wounded,' he says, scared, and sits down.
>
> Sessions takes charge. We still pepper the hedge to discourage fresh attacks, and every once in a while I hear his voice directing the men. My own voice is almost gone. I feel beastly sick. My mouth is full of water or blood. I cough and it is very unpleasant.
>
> He rips the field dressing from my tunic. With considerable skill he wraps the lint about my jaw and throat.[107]

Thwaites' difficulties were only just beginning however, as whilst he was receiving attention in the bottom of the trench, an enormous shell pitched nearby, burying him. It was only with difficulty that he was dug out and eventually returned to the rear. Later, he recalled:

> Apparently my wounds were such that I had no business to be alive at all; famous surgeons would come and have a look at the gaping rent that extended from the point of

> the jaw to a hole under my ear. It was surmised that a brace of machine-gun bullets had hit me.[108]

Following the determined efforts of the Germans to take Messines on 1 November, Frederick Coleman came across an ambulance full of wounded troopers of the Queen's Bays. Over the preceding days and weeks these British soldiers had developed at least a grudging respect for their enemy:

> I asked one of them if he had seen any Germans. 'Loads of em', was the reply. 'Brave beggars, that lot. Three of us were in a house facing the square. Close behind us, a few yards down the street, was our barricade. We saw the Germans start another charge from clear across the open. We pumped a few rounds into 'em, and as they came on we hooked it for the barricade. When those chaps came round the corner where we could get a pot at 'em, how many do you think they was? Just eight! It seemed a pity to kill the plucky mugs, eight of 'em ! Just think of it! Charging like as if they was a whole damn army. I wouldn't minded takin' 'em, but we couldn't. It wouldn't 'a done. Besides, maybe they wouldn't. So we wiped 'em off.' 'But' – he shook his head sagely as he climbed aboard the ambulance – 'they was plucky beggars, if they was Germans. I don't want to see no pluckier. They've been killed off like pigs up there, in that town, and they keep on comin'. They fight stiff, that lot – they fight damn stiff! [109]

The enemy held the northern part of Messines now, and having broken the British line on the ridge to the north, they were starting to move westwards past the town; British troops meanwhile were still hanging on in the south-west corner. The Germans could be seen digging in the open, near a windmill on Messines Ridge. The 7th Cavalry Brigade had been forced to abandon the Zandvoorde Ridge, also losing Hollebeke and Wytschaete. Near the latter, the 12th Lancers made a bayonet charge, an operation so unorthodox for a cavalry regiment that one of them, Private Frank Field wrote home to describe it:

> The cavalry has been used for supporting the infantry in the trenches, and it was that way we got into a bayonet charge. We were supporting the London Scottish, and we heard they would probably be making the charge, so our commanding officer gave orders to join them. Just fancy cavalrymen charging with bayonets! I have never run so fast in my life, and was surprised to find I was not so short-winded as I thought I was. Well, I give the good old London Scottish credit for the way they went about it, considering they were in the firing line for the first time. It was terrible. It didn't last long, the scrap didn't, but I was glad when we dropped into the German trenches and they ran. They can't stick it long, these Germans.
>
> What Tommy doesn't do with his rifle and bayonet, he does with his fists. You get glimpses of chaps punching and wrestling after having had their rifles knocked out of their hands. Since that, I have been in nothing really exciting. It is rotten sticking in the trenches for two or three days, with only shells whizzing over one's head, with only an occasional shot being fired. The German snipers are good, and they very rarely miss, but they are well concealed and it is hard to locate them.
>
> The greatest drawback here is the weather. We have had very few fine days since we have been in the trenches, and everything gets smothered in clay and mud, but the 'boys' are relieved as often as possible and then they go

to billets for a well-earned rest. Of course, the infantry get the better of us, having no horses to look after.

When I left the regiment about three weeks ago, the horses were looking fat and well, and in fine condition, and as fresh as daisies. I am pleased to say they are well looked after and so are the men. The man who says he is not well-looked after and made as comfortable as possible must be unfortunate, and in a badly-managed regiment. But there are very few chaps who can say truthfully that they are not well clad and fed. The food is exceptionally good and plentiful, and all the chaps of my regiment are in the pink.[110]

Major
E. Crawley

12th Lancers, He served with great distinction in West Africa and in the South African War

Major Eustace Crawley, 12th Lancers, killed in action on 2 November 1914. He is commemorated on the Menin Gate at Ypres. (Author's Collection)

Trooper Bolingbroke again wrote home to Oxford to describe the situation:

> We have had two more days in the trenches since then, and had rather a rough day on November 3rd. We were in the front trenches, and there was absolutely nothing between us and the enemy. We are attached to the 1st Cavalry Division, under General de Lisle. The general was very pleased with us, and told our colonel that in future he should not regard us as Territorials, but treat us exactly the same as his other regiments, which was the highest praise he could give us.
>
> The German shell fire is pretty awful, especially some of their shells which our men call 'coal boxes'. They do singularly little damage, however, especially if one keeps good fire, and we do this all right. We have only lost one officer and one trooper and several men wounded up to the present. We are being used as infantry ... and often don't see our horses for days at a time. We march up to the trenches under cover of darkness and relieve the troops therein, and are in turn relieved the next night after 24 hours in them. We then go back to the horses, have day's rest, and then up again, and so on, ad lib!
>
> We get plenty of food, even up in the firing line. We carry tinned rations, and sometimes we manage to get a 'dixie' of tea up. One day, while we were digging some support trenches in the rear, we were near a deserted farm house; we were in clover that day, for we obtained a large pan of most excellent cream, a barrel of cider, dripping, etc, and in the evening some of our fellows made ripping stew out of bully beef and a miscellaneous collection of vegetables from the kitchen garden. It went down jolly topping. We are getting quite expert digging trenches; it

> is, of course, jolly cold o'nights now, especially in the trenches with nothing but greatcoat, but we are very well hardened down now.[111]

On 5 November the attacks fell against the positions of the 16th Lancers. Major C.M. Dixon, in temporary command of the regiment, was killed here, one of his brother officers writing of him:

> He was acting most gallantly at the time he was shot, rallying some French who were next to us, and behaving in the splendid way that always stamped him as the very best. The example set is one that all might envy.[112]

Whilst a soldier of the regiment, writing to Dixon's mother added:

> Major Dixon ran along the trench, telling us to stick it out and show what we were made of, and, as all of us were very fond of him, we did stick it out.[113]

Corporal Charles Dorcas, another soldier of this regiment, was also a witness to these events, writing to his brother:

> The first day we had the pleasure of being under their shellfire for twelve hours – talk about being bombarded, it wasn't in it. When it got dusk they stopped that, and then gave us a nice night of rifle fire. That was alright until dawn the next day (Guy Fawkes Day) when we received a worse shelling than ever. It is only providence that I am alive to tell you about it.
>
> There wasn't a man in those trenches who didn't make light of it. Although they knew that they might get blown to bits any moment. Well, we had twelve hours of it that day. We lost two officers, the CO and a captain. A lance-

> corporal, who was killed, had already been recommended for the DCM for breaking through a barricade with his feet muffled and bringing in wounded. I doubt whether there is a man in the regiment who wouldn't face death smiling. I am proud to be a 16th Lancer.
>
> Our commanding officer came along the line of trenches under heavy shell fire with a can of rifle oil, and when he got to our trench one of the fellows said, 'Wouldn't it be better to pass the can along sir, and get down under cover?' He said, 'Yes, I think I will', and when he got in the trench he begged a pipe of tobacco as he had left his pouch elsewhere. He then went on to say how well the men were sticking it, and what stout hearts they had, and just as he was leaving he said, 'Goodbye boys, and good luck.'
>
> About ten minutes later he was hit in several places by some ___ snipers. Our adjutant stood over him as he lay on the ground (so I have been told since) and took aim with a revolver and fired, hitting one. Poor Major Dixon died the same night. What a loss, one of the bravest of the brave. There wasn't a man in the regiment who wouldn't have followed him to certain death if need be. In fact, every officer in the regiment is liked by the men.[114]

The French poured in attacks to try to retake Wytschaete and ultimately drive the Germans back from Messines. 1st and 2nd Cavalry Brigades were also to join the attack on the latter, from the south-west. Frederick Coleman at 1st Cavalry Brigade HQ was again a witness to the events in this area, and noted:

> the arrival of Lieutenant Chance of the 4th Dragoon Guards. The boy was covered from head to foot with dirt, as though he had rolled in a mud bath. His hand had been

Major C.M. Dixon, 16th Lancers, killed in action on 5 November 1914. He was in temporary command of the regiment at the time, and was killed in the trenches near Ypres, having previously fought at Mons, the Marne, and Aisne battles. (Author's Collection)

painfully smashed by a shrapnel bullet. He came in to report that he had been compelled to pull his squadron back from the line to a position not far behind it. Chance was one of the many junior officers who were in senior positions in those days of heavy casualties. His squadron had been on the right of our line…

His task was the holding of the soft sandy ground that had been so shell-swept the day before. Digging a deep trench line, his lot 'sat tight' under a bombardment that had been terrific. A senior officer on the left of that position told me later in the day that for thirty-five minutes the bursting shells over Chance's squadron formed a curtain of fire that hid from sight the windmill just beyond. Eight, sixteen, twenty-four, and then again eight, sixteen, twenty-four came the Black Marias in line. The ground in front of the trench was thrown up as by a series of mines. Then close behind the trench line, eight, sixteen, twenty-four, until the soft ground caved in in all directions and no trenches were left. Men were buried alive in squads.

Digging out those who had not been buried so deeply as to be hopelessly immured, Chance led his men back, through a hell of shrapnel fire, to the protection of a road-bank a little to the rear. Not a rifle was unchoked, and some time had to be spent in cleaning them. Wiping the sand and dirt from their mouths and eyes, they cheerfully followed the young officer up to the ruins of their trenches and began digging themselves in again. Once more the German howitzers were turned on them, and once more they were buried in their obliterated trenches. Again Chance took the remnants of his squadron back to the road-bank. Realising the futility of further effort to hold the line where the trenches had been, he adopted the new position and improved it as best he could for defence. The wound in his hand, received during the early part of the morning, became so painful he came back to get it dressed, but before seeking the doctor he called on Mullins to acquaint the General of what had taken place, and to apologise for having to give up the part of the line that had been assigned to him.

Chance was only one of many youngsters who showed such mettle. Truly an army containing a multitude of youths of that mould may be well termed invincible. The lads among the officers were given full opportunity in the Messines fighting to show their worth. The few days on that front cost the 1st Cavalry Division seventeen officers killed and sixty wounded.[115]

This of course was the same Roger Chance who had been with the regiment since its first action at Mons, and who would lose an arm as a result of his active service in the war. He was to be awarded the Military Cross and Mentioned in Dispatches twice. Later inheriting a baronetcy, as Sir Roger Chance he was to become active in politics and diplomacy in the interwar years.

Earlier in the campaign, B Squadron of the South Irish Horse had been assigned to duties as I Corps Cavalry; this had largely involved guarding prisoners and searching woods for German stragglers during the days following the Marne and Aisne battles. However, in late October they were used as a mobile reserve, being deployed to support the Connaught Rangers on the Menin Road, and then 3rd Cavalry Brigade at Hollebeke and latterly the infantry of 1st Division at Hooge. Finally, in early November they returned to lines of communication duties. One soldier in B Squadron South Irish Horse, identified only as 'Christy' wrote:

> Just a line to say I received cigarettes and underclothing today. I can assure you they came in very nicely. We are still pounding away at the chaps with the spiked helmets. We expect some big things shortly. Our hardy Irishmen are the boys when hard work and fighting are required. We are sticking to our work like Trojans. Our commanding officer is a thorough gentleman. It is hard to steal a letter through giving graphic details, as we chaps cannot say much. We must let our officers see our correspondence. But I have some good yarns to tell if I get through this lot. Do the people at home ever think of the poor Belgians? They are game fighters; but the poor women and children that are left here. I pity them, lying around their ruined homes that once were happy. They are really frantic with grief; their husbands, brothers, fathers all gone to their lonely graves.

> We are suffering greatly from cold and want of clothes. I got neither boots nor uniform since I came out, but I helped myself to a pair of boots from a dead Frenchman the other night, as it is better to have good boots than bad ones. We have lost a good deal of our fellows with sickness, but with regard to wounds not much.
>
> We are in and out of the trenches daily, always standing to arms. Big guns are going night and day, and the usual list of casualties. I pity our dear old friends our horses, shivering and starved, but we will bear all to clip the claws of the German eagle. I must say the dear old French people treated us very well, but you can see nothing but women in mourning for their dear ones. I am writing this note in an old transport wagon, in the cold and rain.[116]

Its counterpart, the North Irish Horse meanwhile had provided details for police and road control duties behind the lines. Trooper Robert Averall of this unit, writing to a friend at Magherafelt on 2 November stated:

> We are having badly needed rest just now, as our horses were nearly played out. Cavalry is not much use in the trenches, but we hope to get plenty of work when the Germans get on the move again, and I hope the next halt will be in Berlin. It is hardly likely we will be home for Christmas but I hope will be there for the 'Twelfth!' Four Cookstown fellows are here in my troop – Sergeant Ashcroft, Corporal Espie, Lance-Corporal Henry, and Trooper Willie Crooks. We are visited by the enemy's aeroplanes almost every day. They fly over our lines and drop bombs all over the place but do not do much damage, and we usually manage to bring them down in the end. We were on guard during the King's visit, and were on the look-

> out for spies. We succeeded in capturing two disguised as shepherds. They had some sheep and a dog. We are getting tired of mutton chops, so we will perhaps try dog-flesh for a change! Remember me to all the comrades in the U.V.F. and tell them I am hoping to re-join their ranks soon.[117]

On 3 November the final elements of the Leicestershire Yeomanry had arrived in France; shortly afterwards, after just a day or two to rest their horses, they commenced duty as the general reserve of the 7th Cavalry Brigade. Sergeant Charles C. Bailey was from Hoby, and commanded the Rutland Troop, part of A Squadron, Leicestershire Yeomanry. He described events from his perspective in a heavily censored letter, published in his local newspaper:

> After about three hours, we proceeded to ___ and bivouacked. We could now hear the sound of guns, and naturally expected we were working our way to the firing line. Every day was getting colder, but were lucky in getting a farm barn to sleep in, with plenty of straw. After being here for a few days, we had orders to join the ___, which consists of the 1st and 2nd Life Guards, and proceed the front. We marched to ____, and bivouacked there for the night. It rained the whole day long, and our cloaks and kit hung like buckets of water on our shoulders. The night was horribly cold and wet. We all slept in an empty house, on bare floor. There was a tremendous cannonade of guns going on, and we knew we must be getting very close to the firing line.
>
> The fire from the guns lit the darkness. There was a cavalry regiment of Algerians staying here, too. Reveille was at 4 a.m., and we marched off 6 a.m. to Ypres. We had pass through Ypres under fire. The town had been bombarded for 24 hours, and was burning. It was a horrible

sight to see this beautiful town in ruins and flames, and we never saw a single person in it as we passed through. A little further on, one of the British guns went off just by the side of the road close to us. We nearly jumped out of our saddles with such a sudden shock. We bivouacked about two miles out, and were under shell fire the whole night. This was our first experience of fire, and [we] did not like the whistling of the shells going over our heads. The S Battery of the Royal Horse Artillery were in the same field, and were jolly good mates for us. Sleeping in front of our horses in the open. The 1st and 2nd Life Guards were in the trenches at the time. We spent the next day digging trenches to get ourselves under cover, and had just about finished when we were ordered to take ourselves up in the firing line.

We all turned out except a few who were left in charge of our horses. We started off at dusk, and had to tramp through mud and water nearly up to our knees with our cloaks dragging on the ground like a lady's dress. The amount of kit we had to carry made it very hard work. Shells were dropping all around, and as we neared the firing line we had our first experience of bullets whizzing over our heads. On looking round on several occasions at our long queue as we marched in half-sections, I could not help but laugh. You may imagine every man kept very low, and, in spite of water and mud, was very often on his hands and knees. I can tell you I was myself. There was not a word, only whisper. We tramped along, and finally got there, and were ordered to form the support. There were not enough trenches for all, so the unfortunate ones had to begin to dig themselves in, and I can tell you they were not long in doing so. [Excision by Censor.] We were in a thick wood, and had a splendid position. [Further excision.][118]

1984 Trooper Freeman F. Bowley, Leicestershire Yeomanry, who arrived in France on 2 November 1914. (Author's Collection)

Trooper Horace W. Breeze was with B Squadron of the same regiment, and writing from the front to friends in Leicester, described the events of the preceding days when the regiment was in action for the first time:

> This line or two I write just to take advantage of a hard-earned chance. At last we are resting after a fortnight in the thick of it, around ___ where the greatest battle of the war is raging. In the trenches, which we occupied together with the 1st and 2nd Life Guards and the Coldstream Guards, the water was nearly knee deep, and the roads to them the same depth in mud. For a fortnight we have

been in the trenches periodically, wet through and no chance of a change. I took my boots off for the first time for three weeks on Tuesday, and have not been able to walk since. We are, to a man, footsore, and ill-health is very prevalent, but after a few days rest no doubt all will be fit again.

The mud and water was relieved a few days ago by heavy snow, severe winter weather. In the trenches under either conditions it is awful—one dare not go to sleep, for when waking, one finds every limb frozen beyond feeling. Of course, then it only takes a sally on the enemy's side to make us warm. The Life Guards and Coldstream have lost very heavily, but the Yeomanry, I think, are the luckiest regiment at the front, having only three wounded. The Guards say we have been most lucky. A week ago we had 30 of our horses killed, and not one man was hurt. We were all asleep in a large house about 300 yards away. The shell fire is appalling, and unceasing day and night. On the march or bivouacked we are heavily bombarded. We pass, en route, many grim sights, which force home the cruel, murderous and inhuman aspects of this war. It is beyond the greatest imagination – it must be seen – just one glance. It is frightful to see the fine old churches and historic buildings and peasants' homes all laid low by German guns. We are all well supplied with tobacco and cigarettes, and we are just in receipt of some underclothing from the Queen and 'the Women of the Empire'. There is one thing we all crave for but cannot get for anything, that is chocolate. There will be no good old Christmas at home for us this year, but let us hope that this terrible carnage will be cut short by a crushing defeat to our enemies.[119]

On 5 November the 6th Cavalry Brigade went into the trenches at Heronthage Wood, east of Ypres and on the following day the Germans shelled the front line with great intensity. Trooper G.W. Davis, 10th Hussars, part of this brigade, wrote to his family on 7 November of an incident which occurred here the previous evening:

> I am the luckiest coon alive, pieces of German shrapnel splintering all round, and I am only getting a few severe headaches. We relieved an infantry regiment in the trenches and remained there for thirty hours. We were only 350 yards from the German lines, and could plainly see their tin helmets, which make fine marks.
>
> As evening wore on the enemy made a desperate attack on us, shelling us with shrapnel, maxims, and rifle fire, and our little lot retaliating same like. Whilst this lasted (ten to twelve hours) it was real hellish, but our chaps were real lucky, losing practically no one.
>
> To keep one's head above a trench to watch any movement in front while shrapnel is bursting all around is a risky concern. We cannot do much mounted work out here, owing to the woody nature of the country. It's rather a good job for the Kaiser's lot, as our chaps are longing for a gallop. It might come later though, and then – goodness help them!
>
> These beggars have all sorts of devices when attacks are coming off. Last night they were using star lights to illuminate our position, and we had to be pretty nippy in dodging their bullets. But they cannot get over our doggedness, which completely upsets them. I am in the best of health and spirits, considering the time; but oh! for a change, a wash and something nice to eat![120]

By 15 November Archibald Home recorded that winter had now arrived in earnest and that they had had their first really cold day;

Captain A.W. Macarthur-Onslow, 16th Lancers, killed by a shell in the trenches near Ypres on 5 November 1914. (Author's Collection)

snow had fallen throughout and it had been a wretched day for the men in the trenches; roads had been turned into mud baths. Morale however remained high. On the following day he wrote:

> Our 2nd Cavalry [Brigade] got out of the trenches at 2am and were very dirty but very cheerful. They were in a wood, with the German trenches 50 yards away – the trees between them had been levelled down by the shells which had burst and formed an impenetrable abattis. We are keeping them out tonight and they go back tomorrow.[121]

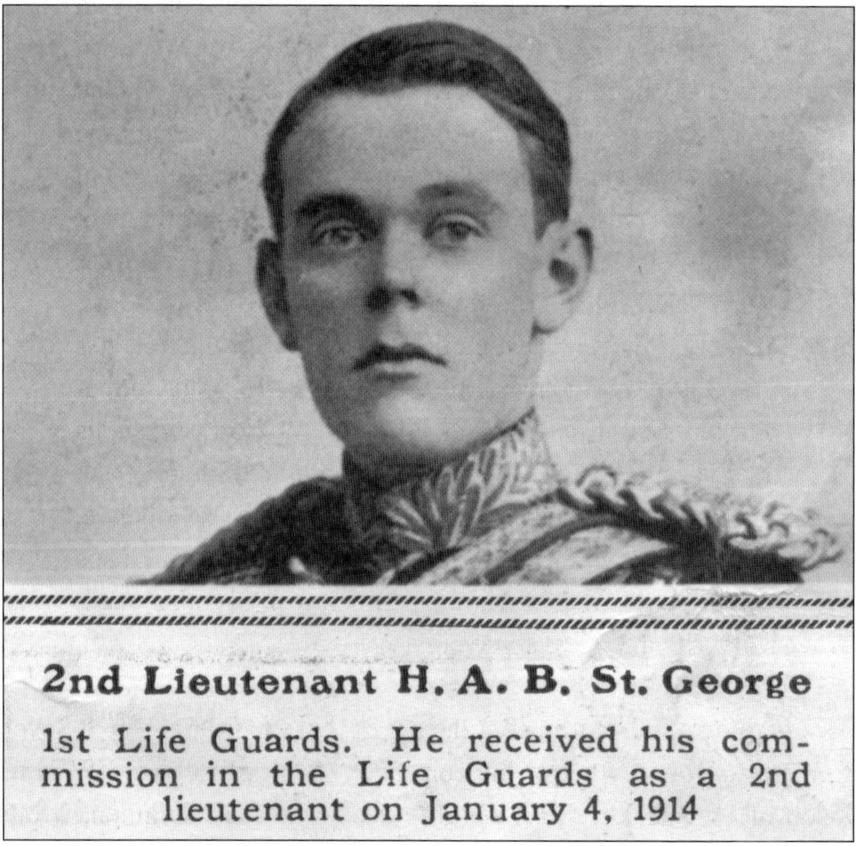

Second Lieutenant Howard Avenel Bligh St George, 1st Life Guards, who died on 15 November 1914. He is buried in Zillebeke Churchyard. (Author's Collection)

The fighting around Ypres stuttered on through November, with the Yeomanry units attached to each cavalry brigade taking their share of the burden. A pathetic letter came from Trooper Albert Edward Pool, of the North Somerset Yeomanry, who before the war had been assistant honorary secretary to the Weston-super-Mare and Banwell Horse and Agricultural Association. Pool was wounded at Ypres on 17 November 1914, and the letter was received by his parents at Weston-super-Mare shortly afterwards. Writing from the hospital at Rouen just before he underwent an operation, Trooper Pool said:

> I expect [to] be operated on this afternoon and have shell fragments removed. I was hit at 2.50, and lay in the trenches until 8.30 the same night on wet, sodden ground—bleeding. But here we are again. In my trench there was my pal on the right. He was shot through the head. Then Dick Wilson on my left, yelling 'Come on, my bonny lads! My Somerset boys' and the next moment he was shot through the forehead, dead. There were only 'Mac' Shepherd and Sergeant Smith left with me. Lionel Brown and seven others found me in the trenches eventually, and carried me on eight rifles about three-quarters of a mile, black as night, awful road, and shells all over the place. It was one continual fall of 'Jack Johnsons' and shrapnel shells all the time… Goodbye. Don't worry about me. I am in good hands, and perhaps will be sent home, of which I shall glad. Remember to all, and write and send some cigarettes, please.[122]

Trooper Pool died shortly after the operation, and is buried at St Sever Cemetery, Rouen. One of his comrades, Trooper Reginald Weight, a son of Mr and Mrs B.C. Weight of Wood Street, Swindon, wrote home in a similar vein. This young soldier at the outbreak of war was employed as a clerk in the Education Offices at Weston-super-Mare, and had given up a good position to join the North Somerset Yeomanry. He was attached to B Squadron, and after only five weeks training had been ordered to the front with his regiment. From news which had filtered through to Swindon it was clear that his regiment had been in the fighting in the Ypres area. In his letter Trooper Weight acknowledged the receipt of welcome gifts sent him by his father and mother, and referred to the fact that all the letters sent to them or despatched from the front were censored, thus accounting for the delay in transmission. He added:

> We have found it very cold. It snowed here for the first time last Wednesday (Nov. 18th) and it has been freezing ever since. The only way to keep warm is to be cheery and be always on the move, but alas! to be cheery is hard at times. I should like a pair of woollen gloves and a scarf, if you would send them out. I had a wash and a shave—the first wash for about a week. I believe my last shave was about 10 days ago, and I had a frightful growth. I shall be ever so pleased to receive some chocolate. Please send a plain kind – 'Menier' for instance – it serves as a nourishment as well, then. Before I close I think it only right to tell you – you will no doubt read about it – that our regiment has been in action. I lost several good chums, but Anderson and I came through.[123]

Another soldier of the Queen's Own Oxfordshire Hussars, Trooper Tom Stone, had a good knowledge of French and this was of great help to him and his comrades in A Squadron, in dealing with the local inhabitants for extra food. At this time of year his thoughts inevitably turned to the festive season:

> At present we are having rather an easy time, although there is still plenty to do, even when we are supposed

> to be resting. Lately it has been very wet, making our horse lines in an awful mess, and for the last two or three days we have been busy carting the mud away. At night we have nothing to do but sit and talk, or sing. We sleep in barns, on the hay or straw, and are very comfortable at night. —, the nearest town, is about four miles away. Yesterday, one of the fellows in our set went and bought a good stock of fresh meat, and butter, etc, which enables us to have a nice little feed at night. When we first came here we occasionally were able to buy a duck, or a fowl, but now the people won't sell them, so we have to fall back on our own resources.
>
> Around here the fighting has slackened in intensity, the weather no doubt having a good deal to do with it. A few of the senior non-commissioned officers are having leave, but I don't expect we shall get any. I should like to get home just for Christmas, as it will be the first time I have ever missed spending Christmas at home. I am afraid there will be many as unhappy Christmas spent this time in Belgium and France, and I am glad that the people in England are doing something for them.[124]

Shortly after the close of the First Battle of Ypres, Sir John French, commander of the BEF, addressed members of a number of Yeomanry regiments for about a quarter of an hour, congratulating them on their recent endeavours. In the course of his speech he referred to their coolness under fire, and asserted that their performance had been as good as that of the best trained regular cavalry. During the period from 31 October to 5 November when they held the line against overwhelming odds, their performance was particularly valuable, indeed he described this as one of the greatest feats of the war. Almost breaking down at times, French commiserated with them over the misfortunes of war and the losses that they had suffered, but also extolled their patriotism in volunteering for active service so early in the campaign when others in Britain were still thinking about it. It was a fitting tribute to the sacrifice of these part time cavalrymen.

After a short but unpleasant spell in the trenches in front of Wulverghem, facing Messines, the glad news came through on 19 November that the 12th Lancers were to go into reserve for three weeks, a welcome thought now that the damp Flemish winter had turned to frosty and cold conditions, defined by the intense clarity of the air. One officer, Lieutenant J. Leslie, wrote on 22 November:

> We had by this time become pretty hardened to rapid disillusionments, but it was a disappointing moment when only a few hours later we got the order to move up and take over a portion of the trench in the French area ... and the blinding snowstorm which set in just as we moved off did not add to our appreciation of the situation. Nor indeed did the condition of the trenches. For the French, no more than forty yards from the Germans and exhausted by three weeks' continuous fighting, had been too tired even to bury their dead or repair their defences. My trench had from 16 to 18 inches of water in it, a clay bottom and no straw. The first thing I fell over was a dead man. There were three others, two still unburied, and one buried in the bottom of the trench. There was only one place where it was possible to stand upright, and owing to the water we could not lie down. As we cavalry do not have packs and blankets you can imagine our prospects for the next 24 hours were not exactly rosy. ... We did not allow the men to sleep. We should never have been able to wake them in time if they had been rushed, and moreover they would have been frostbitten if they had slept. ... We stood most of the night marking time in the mud and water and with our backs bent to keep our heads down. ...'[125]

Captain Clement Henry Peto, 10th Hussars, who was shot through the head and killed in the line between Hooge and Zillebeke on 17 November 1914. He is buried in Ypres Town Cemetery. (Author's Collection)

Captain C. H. Peto
10th Hussars. He joined the Hussars in February, 1904, and became a captain in September, 1910

Trooper W. Page of the 2nd Life Guards, in a letter dated 23 November, wrote to his sister-in-law of the lack of shelter when in the line and the worsening weather:

> We have been in the thickest of the fighting round Ypres. It was like being in hell, if there is one. We were under shell fire for days at a time. The Germans made several attacks on our trenches, but were repulsed every time with great loss. We let them get only a few yards from our trenches and then opened fire on I them. I expect you read all about this in the papers. We are having plenty of frost and snow, and so cold at nights. I have never felt it so before. We were without any shelter for five days, but, thank goodness, we have found a barn with a little straw in, and only two shell holes in the top. It was as good as a first-class house out here.
>
> The Germans have been shelling a town near here and killing a lot of the people who had not shifted, and two churches went west, also a few graves in the churchyard. The holes were about 7ft. deep. The people are very good to us out here, and we are having plenty of clothes and cigarettes sent us, so there is nothing I want just now. If any of my letters get into the 'Oxfordshire Weekly News' I should like to see it. I saw Ben Howard the other day, and he was all right. Sorry I shall not be home for

12549 Trooper John A. Palmer was a Boer War veteran, who volunteered for the 11th Hussars in 1914. He reached the unit in mid-November. This photo neatly illustrates the way that cavalry uniform had evolved to meet the conditions, with 'Gor Blimey' trench cap, and a bayonet on a waist belt accompanying the riding crop. (Author's Collection)

> Christmas, but I am quite happy. This is a fine game out here shooting at live targets! We are about to take up a new position, which is a hot corner I've been told.[126]

In another letter to a friend, dated about the same time, Trooper Page added:

> We have come from Ypres, where the fighting is very fierce; in fact, we lost more men out of our regiment this last four weeks than we did in any other big fight. We have been in the advance trenches for two and three days at a time, also several attacks which were made by the Germans were held back by the cavalry regiments. In the front of our trenches there were hundreds of dead and wounded, and at night they did kick up a row. We dare not put our heads over the trench or we should get picked off. The French artillery are playing hell with them, and their trenches are going up in the air by the black shells. As I write this letter the noise of guns and rifle fire is sounding all round me, and a trainload of wounded are about to start away for the base hospitals. The towns and villages all about here are in ruins, and the snow is on the ground. I have seen Ben Howard, as the Oxford Yeomanry have taken our place in the 4th Brigade, and he is all right. It is much colder out here than in England, and at night the frost—oh dear! I wish I was down in the bottom room at the club talking about war.[127]

Trooper Gilbert Tiptod of B Squadron of the Leicestershire Yeomanry, writing to his family in a letter dated 'Near Cassel 8 December', added a melancholy valediction:

> I shall be pleased to receive any eatables, but you need not trouble about clothes, we get any amount of them.

> Please pack the things up well as the parcels get torn open before we get them … Ypres is a fine place, or rather was. Since we left it they have shelled it to the ground. They used to shell it every day because they were unable to take it. It is almost deserted.[128]

The city that so many British soldiers had already given their lives to defend had already become a symbolic casualty, epitomising the destruction and devastation of this war. It was a grim and bitter end to a campaign which had started in the heat and dust of high summer, in which along with the weather, tactics and fighting conditions had altered immeasurably; yet despite the hardships and the losses the exhausted British cavalry knew that their line had held, Ypres and the Channel ports had been saved, and – for now – the Germans had been kept at bay.

Epilogue

It is often the case now that the British soldiers of the First World War are portrayed as victims, and without agency; the often unwilling passive participants in events beyond their control. The British cavalry of 1914 however disproves this thesis. An élite force, possessed of great *esprit de corps* they acted with initiative and purpose throughout those months, their professional pride being self-evident.

The striking irony of the experience of the British cavalry in 1914 however lay in the fact that, before the war, many of its members had held the view that it was only useful in a mounted role. Yet with a few notable exceptions, its performance as a mounted force in the months of August and September 1914 had been somewhat lacklustre. By the same token, many post-war regimental historians regarded the period of trench warfare from October onwards as nothing short of a disaster for the cavalry. It was almost as if serving in the trenches in a dismounted role was seen as something of a disgrace, yet many modern historians would argue that this was in fact the most important contribution of the British cavalry in 1914. The skills of the mounted arm, especially in musketry were equal to if not better than those of the infantry, and they deployed them to great effect.

In particular, the part played by the cavalry in the First Battle of Ypres was nothing short of critical, and it could be argued that the arm was vital in preventing a German breakthrough here, something which would have almost certainly spelled defeat for the allies at this juncture in the war. If the emergence on the battlefield of aeroplanes, motorcars and ultimately tanks would be the writing on the wall for the horse as an instrument of war, then this campaign was indeed a fitting swansong.

Spring 1915, and the funeral at Doberitz PoW camp, Germany of Trooper Charles Bland. Marked with a cross on the left is the sender of this postcard picture, Saddler Frederick Pearce; both men served with the 15th Hussars, and were reported missing in August 1914. (Author's Collection)

Notes

Introduction

1. HMSO, *Cavalry Training 1907*, London, 1907, p187
2. General Sir Horace Smith-Dorrien, *Memories of Forty-Eight Years' Service*, New York, 1925, p359
3. Major General Sir M.F. Rimington, *Our Cavalry*, London, 1912, p17
4. Major General James D. Lunt, *Charge to Glory!*, New York, 1960, pIX
5. Rimington, *Our Cavalry*, p156
6. Op. cit.
7. Rimington, *Our Cavalry*, p165
8. Richard van Emden, *Teenage Tommy,* Pen & Sword Books, Barnsley, 2014, p18

Chapter One

9. Sir Roger Chance, Audio recording, Liddle Collection, University of Leeds, Author's transcript
10. Herbert Maddick, *A Cavalryman at the Front* in *The Cornhill Magazine* Vol. 38 Issue 225, March 1915, p388
11. Maddick, *Cavalryman*, p389
12. Maddick, *Cavalryman*, p391

13. E. Thomas, *I Fired the First Shot!,* in Sir John Hammerton (ed.), *The Great War ... I was There!*, London, n.d., p41
14. T.T. Pitman, *General Outline of Cavalry Operations on the Western Front* in *Cavalry Journal,* Vol. 12, 1922, p28
15. J.C. Darling, *20th Hussars in the Great War*, Lyndhurst, 1923, p10
16. Maddick, *Cavalryman*, p392
17. Van Emden, *Teenage Tommy*, p52
18. Sir Roger Chance, Audio recording, Liddle Collection, University of Leeds, Author's transcript
19. John Buchan, *Francis and Riversdale Grenfell, a Memoir*, London, 1920, p195
20. Harry Easton, Manuscript Recollections, Liddle Collection, University of Leeds
21. James A. Kilpatrick, *Tommy Atkins at War*, New York, 1914, p47
22. *Croydon Times*, 14 November 1914
23. Easton, Manuscript Recollections
24. John Curry et al, *The Diary of a World War 1 Cavalryman: Corporal Robert Waister of the 18th Hussars 1911–1918* sl, 2017, p48
25. Pitman, *General Outline*, p82
26. Buchan, *Francis and Riversdale Grenfell,* p196
27. Alfred W. Pollard, *Two Brothers: Accounts Rendered*, London, 1917, p35
28. Buchan, *Francis and Riversdale Grenfell,* p196
29. *Croydon Times*, 3 October 1914
30. *The Scotsman*, 17 October 1914
31. *Liverpool Echo*, 5 September 1914
32. *Hastings & St Leonards Observer*, 10 October 1914
33. Arthur Osburne, *Unwilling Passenger* London, 1932, p51
34. Ciaran Byrne, *The Harp and Crown* sl, 2007, p57
35. Maddick, *Cavalryman*, p394

Chapter Two

36. Maddick, *Cavalryman*, p396
37. Maddick, *Cavalryman*, p397
38. *Haslingden Gazette*, 17 October 1914
39. *Richmond and Twickenham Times*, 16 January 1915
40. Paul Maze, *A Frenchman in Khaki* London, 1934, p46
41. Walter Temple Willcox, *3rd King's Hussars in the Great War*, London, 1925, p19
42. Charles Burnett *Memoirs of the 18th (Queen Mary's Own) Royal Hussars 1906–1922*, Winchester, 1926, p32
43. *Evening News,* [London], 19 November1914
44. *Dundee Courier*, 23 September 1914
45. *Aberdeen Evening Express*, 22 September 1914
46. *Yorkshire Evening Post*, 19 September 1914
47. Archibald Home*, The Diary of a World War I Cavalry Officer* Tunbridge Wells, 1985, p26
48. Frederick Coleman, *From Mons to Ypres With French*, New York 1916, p93
49. William Clarke, Manuscript Recollections, Liddle Collection, University of Leeds
50. Lionel E. Blackburne, *Charles (Lieutenant Colonel C.E. Blackburne DSO 5th Dragoon Guards): A Memoir,* London 1919, p147
51. H.M. Hill, unpublished papers, Liddle Collection, University of Leeds
52. https://www.stadt-land-oldenburg.de/i_weltkrieg.htm (Author's translation)

Chapter Three

53. *Dublin Daily Express*, 23 October 1914
54. *Yorkshire Evening News*, 6 October 1914

55. Sir Jock Crabbe, unpublished typescript recollections, Liddle Collection, University of Leeds
56. Op. cit.
57. Op. cit.
58. Coleman, *From Mons to Ypres*, p112
59. Osburne, *Unwilling Passenger*, p117
60. Charles Burnett, *Memoirs of the 18th Royal Hussars,* Winchester, 1926, p43
61. Burnett, *Memoirs*, p44
62. Journal of the 5th Inniskilling Dragoon Guards, 1935, p127
63. Op. cit.
64. *The People*, 20 October 1914
65. Crabbe, recollections
66. Op. cit.
67. *Ramsey Courier* 2, October 1914
68. Captain P.F. Stewart, *History of the XII Royal Lancers,* London, 1950, p257
69. Stewart, *History of the XII Royal Lancers*, p257
70. Stewart, *History of the XII Royal Lancers*, p258
71. *Preston Herald*, 28 November 1914
72. Van Emden, *Teenage Tommy,* p74
73. *Saffron Walden Weekly News*, 9 October 1914
74. Osburne, *Unwilling Passenger*, p132
75. Osburne, *Unwilling Passenger*, p136
76. *Londonderry Sentinel*, 28 November 1914
77. Maddick, *Cavalryman,* p412
78. Home, *Diary,* p25

Chapter Four

79. John Cusack, *Scarlet Fever A Lifetime with Horses*, London, 1972, p46
80. Op. cit.

81. Stewart, *History of the XII Royal Lancers,* p260
82. *Evening Mail*, (London), 30 October 1914
83. Home, *Diary*, p30
84. Stewart, *History of the XII Royal Lancers*, p262
85. T.L. Horn, unpublished typescript recollections, Liddle Collection, University of Leeds
86. *Regimental Journal of the 9th/12th Royal Lancers (Prince of Wales's)*, 2001, Vol. XI. No, 4
87. S.C. Dumbreck, unpublished manuscript diary, Liddle Collection, University of Leeds

Chapter Five

88. Buchan, *Francis and Riversdale Grenfell,* p213
89. Home, *Diary*, p33
90. *Worthing Gazette*, 9 December 1914
91. *Belfast Telegraph*, 20 November 1914
92. *Northampton Chronicle and Echo,* 25 November 1914
93. Norman Graham Thwaites, *Velvet and Vinegar,* London, 1932, p96
94. https://secondlifeguards.wordpress/com/category/191410/.
95. *Memorials of Rugbeians who fell in the Great War,* Vol. 1, Medici Society Ltd, 1916
96. *Dublin Daily Express,* 9 November 1914
97. Op. cit.
98. *Bury Times*, 7 November 1914
99. Op cit
100. *Banbury Advertiser*, 26 November 1914
101. Op. cit.
102. *Shields Daily News*, 11 November 1914
103. Blackburne, *Charles*, p153
104. *Coalville Times*, 13 November 1914
105. *South Yorkshire Times*, 5 December 1914
106. Op. cit.

107. Thwaites, *Velvet and Vinegar,* p107
108. Thwaites, *Velvet and Vinegar*, p116
109. Coleman, *From Mons to Ypres*, p282
110. *Richmond and Twickenham Times*, 16 January 1915
111. *Banbury Advertiser*, 26 November 1914
112. *Memorials of Rugbeians*
113. Op. cit.
114. *Evening News*, [London], 19 November 1914
115. Coleman, *From Mons to Ypres,* p299
116. *Freeman's Journal*, 24 November 1914
117. *Mid-Ulster Mail*, 12 December 1914
118. *Grantham Journal*, 24 December 1914
119. *Melton Mowbray Mercury*, 3 December 1914
120. *Evening News*, [London], 19 November 1914
121. Home, *Diary*, p39
122. *Dundee Evening Telegraph*, 8 December 1914
123. *North Wiltshire Herald*, 4 December 1914
124. *Bicester Herald*, 18 December 1914
125. Stewart, *History of the XII Royal Lancers*, p267
126. *Oxfordshire Weekly News*, 2 December 1914
127. Op. cit.
128. *Melton Mowbray Mercury and Oakham and Uppingham News*, 17 December 1914

Bibliography

Journal of the 5th Inniskilling Dragoon Guards, 1935

Memorials of Rugbeians who fell in the Great War, Vol. 1, Medici Society Ltd, 1916

Regimental Journal of the 9th/12th Royal Lancers (Prince of Wales's) 2001 Vol. XI No. 4

Anglesey, George Charles Henry Victor Paget, Marquess of, *A History of the British Cavalry 1816–1919 Vol. 7,* London, 1996

Badsey, Stephen *Doctrine and Reform in the British Cavalry 1880-1918* Aldershot, 2008

Blackburne, Lionel E., *Charles (Lieutenant Colonel C.E. Blackburne DSO 5th Dragoon Guards): A Memoir,* London, 1919

Bond, Brian, *Doctrine and Training in the British Cavalry 1870–1914* in M. Howard (ed.), *The Theory and Practice of War,* London, 1965

Buchan, John, *Francis and Riversdale Grenfell, a Memoir* London, 1920

Burnett, Charles, *Memoirs of the 18th (Queen Mary's Own) Royal Hussars 1906–1922,* Winchester, 1926

Byrne, Ciaran *The Harp and Crown, the History of the 5th Royal Irish Lancers 1902–1922,* sl, 2007

Coleman, Frederick *From Mons to Ypres With French,* New York, 1916

Curry, John, et al, *The Diary of a World War 1 Cavalryman: Corporal Robert Waister of the 18th Hussars 1911–1918,* sl, 2017

Cusack, John, *Scarlet Fever A Lifetime with Horses,* London, 1972

Darling, J.C., *20th Hussars in the Great War,* Lyndhurst, 1923

Evans, H.K.D., et al, *The 4th (Queen's Own) Hussars in the Great War,* Aldershot, 1920

HMSO, *Cavalry Training 1907*, London, 1907

Home, Archibald, *The Diary of a World War I Cavalry Officer,* Tunbridge Wells, 1985

Jones, Spencer, *Scouting for Soldiers: Reconnaissance and the British Cavalry 1899–1914* in *War in History,* Vol. 18, No. 4

Kilpatrick, James A., *Tommy Atkins at War, As Told In His Own Letters*, New York, 1914

Lunt, James D., *Charge to Glory!,* New York, 1960

Maddick, Herbert, *A Cavalryman at the Front* in *The Cornhill Magazine,* Vol. 38, Issue 225, March 1915

Maze, Paul, *A Frenchman in Khaki,* London, 1934

Osburn, Arthur, *Unwilling Passenger,* London, 1932

Pitman, T.T., *General Outline of Cavalry Operations on the Western Front* in *Cavalry Journal,* Vol. 12, 1922

Richardson, Matthew, *1914: Voices from the Battlefields,* Pen & Sword Books, Barnsley, 2013

Rimington, Major General M.F., *Our Cavalry* London, 1912

Smith-Dorrien, H., *Memories of Forty-Eight Years' Service,* New York, 1925

Spiers, Edward M., *The British Cavalry 1902–1914* in *Journal of the Society for Army Historical Research*, summer 1979, Vol. 57, No. 230

Stewart, Captain P.F., *The History of the XII Royal Lancers,* London, 1950

Thwaites, Norman Graham *Velvet and Vinegar,* London, 1932

Van Emden, Richard, *Teenage Tommy, Memoirs of a Cavalryman in the First World War* Pen & Sword Books, 2014

Von Poseck, Maximilian, *The German Cavalry 1914 in France & Belgium* (trans. J.W. How), Berlin, 1923

Whitmore, Francis Henry Douglas Charlton, *The 10th (P.W.O.) Hussars and the Essex Yeomanry During the Great War,* Colchester, 1920

Willcox, Walter Temple, *3rd King's Hussars in the Great War,* London, 1925

Index